CAMPAIGN 430

KADESH 1286 BC

Egypt Attempts to Take Syria

ANTHONY SPALINGER ILLUSTRATED BY MARCO CAPPARONI

OSPREY PUBLISHING
Bloomsbury Publishing Plc
Kemp House, Chawley Park, Cumnor Hill, Oxford OX2 9PH, UK
Bloomsbury Publishing Ireland Limited,
29 Earlsfort Terrace, Dublin 2, D02 AY28, Ireland
Bloomsbury Publishing Inc.
1359 Broadway, 12th Floor, New York, NY 10018, USA
E-mail: info@ospreypublishing.com
www.ospreypublishing.com

OSPREY is a trademark of Osprey Publishing Ltd

First published in Great Britain in 2026

A catalogue record for this book is available from the British Library.

ISBN: PB 9781472870551; eBook 9781472870520; ePDF 9781472870537; XML 9781472870544

26 27 28 29 30 10 9 8 7 6 5 4 3 2 1

Maps by Bounford.com
3D BEV by Paul Kime
Index by Fionbar Lyons
Typeset by Lumina Datamatics Ltd
Printed by Repro India Ltd

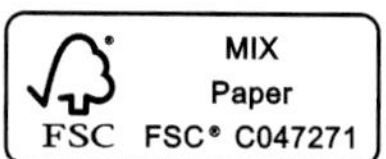

Osprey Publishing supports the Woodland Trust, the UK's leading woodland conservation charity.

To find out more about our authors and books visit **www.ospreypublishing.com**. Here you will find extracts, author interviews, details of forthcoming events and the option to sign up for our newsletter.

For product safety related questions contact productsafety@bloomsbury.com

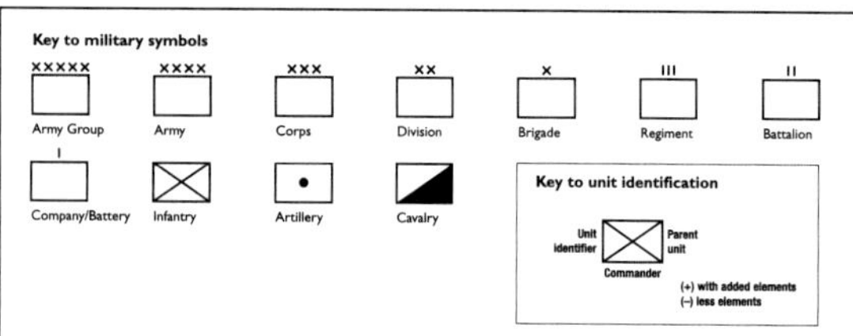

Author's note

In this work the Julian date of 1290 BC has been taken as the accession year of Ramesses II. Hence, the battle of Kadesh, which occurred five years later, is set on 1286 BC. The precise chronology of Ramesses still remains controversial for many as there remains the 'contender,' 1279 BC, for the king's first regnal year. Still, I have preferred the more 'traditional' date. Present non-Egyptological scholarship appears to opt for 1290 BC.

Dedication

To Two Kadesh Enthusiasts, Peter Brand and Claude Obsomer.

Front cover main illustration: Clash of the chariots. (Marco Capparoni)
Title page photograph: Detail of the Hittite chariot warriors. Abydos, north exterior wall, right side. (Courtesy of Claude Obsomer)

CONTENTS

ORIGINS OF THE CAMPAIGN

THE BACKGROUND TO THE HITTITE–EGYPTIAN CONFLICT

The circumstances leading to the crucial military encounter of Pharaoh Ramesses II at Kadesh in Syria (1286 or 1275 BC) must be seen in light of previous attempts by the Egyptians to control the territory of Amurru in southern Syria. Because of its strategic importance, Kadesh had to be regulated by an outside polity of great size and power unless it remained as an independent metropolis spanning the highways of Syria. It oversaw the zone which lay between the highlands and low-lying mountains of central and northern Syria, as well as the south-eastern road entrances to northern Mesopotamia. Kadesh was, as a rule, never subjugated to the status of a mere vassal state having no independence. The treaties that were arranged with the Hittites indicate that so long as the local potentate supported the great king of Hatti in battle, ensured that he dealt effectively with fugitives and never aligned himself to another power, his city-state was left alone.

The site of Kadesh I. A view to the west showing the Orontes River undulating southwards. Note how narrow and shallow it is. (www.HolyLandPhotos.org)

The zone of contention in Syria, Dynasty XIX

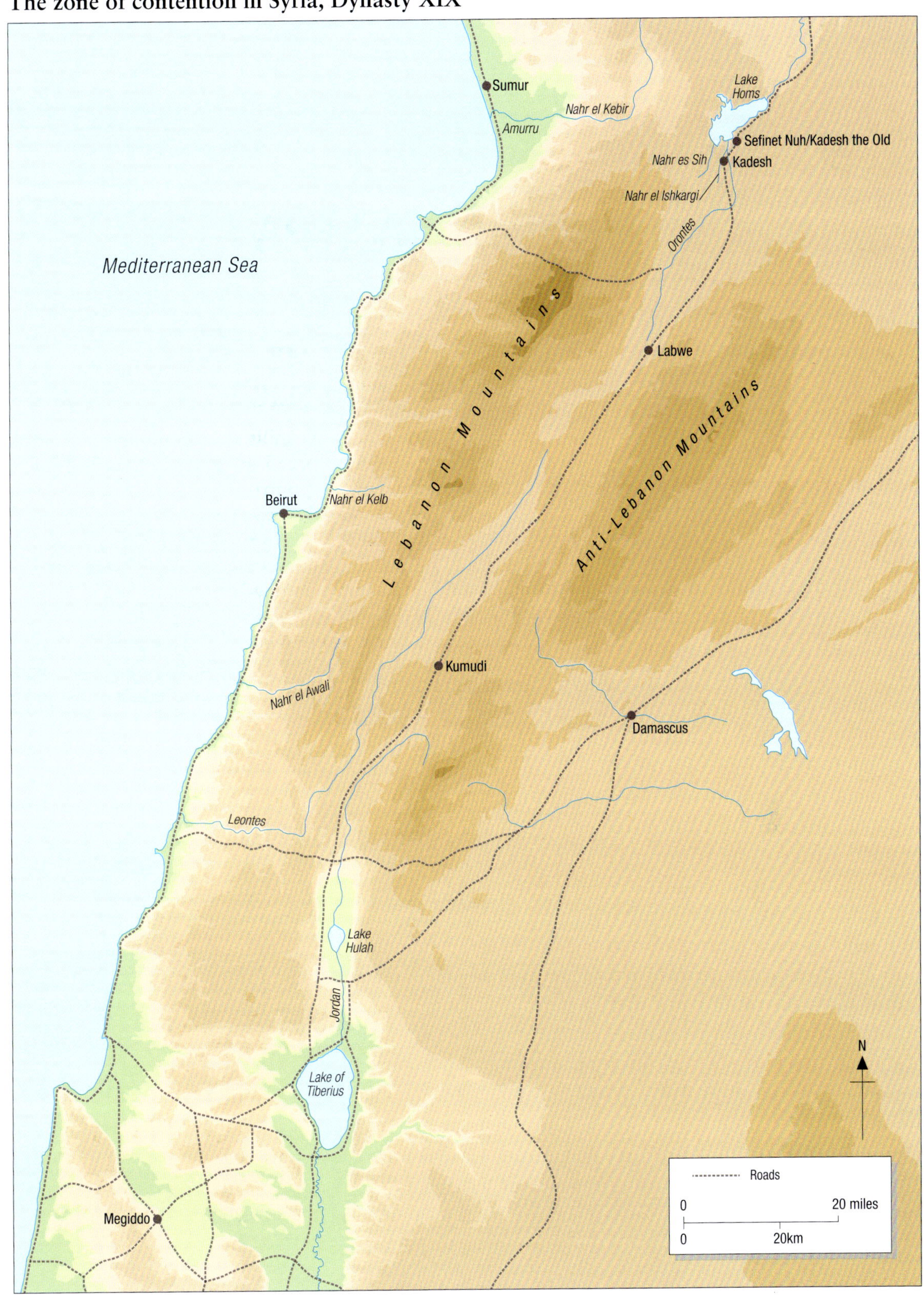

The site of Kadesh II. (Peter Parr, reproduced by permission of Oxbow Books)

Peter Brand has categorized the city as a thorn in the side of the Egyptians. He referred to the march of Thutmose III of mid-Dynasty XVIII into the heartland of Syria. This event, his 'Euphratean campaign', followed up a series of continual military advances into Syria. All had begun in Thutmose III's 22nd regnal year when he dealt with a rebellion in Palestine. The northern city states, centred on Megiddo, revolted at the instigation of the prince of Kadesh, who was dependent upon the ruler of the kingdom of Mitanni, located in the heartland of Syria.

After taking Megiddo, Thutmose proceeded northwards via the King's Highway, which Ramesses II later took. The highway went north of Megiddo through the central valley region of Palestine and southern Syria. Thutmose moved inland northwards to Kadesh and ensured that it remained under Egyptian control. After many years, Kadesh reverted to Mitannian control, only to be seized by the Hittites at the end of Dynasty XVIII.

By the end of Dynasty XVIII, Aziru, the son of Abdi-Ashita of Amurru, expanded his small kingdom to include Ullaza, Ammiya and Irqata. It was Aziru who cemented positive relations with the Hittites under their imperialistic king, Suppiluliuma. The competing alliances and political breaks indicate that by the reign of Seti I, Tyre, Arvad and Beirut – not to mention Byblos – were allied to Amurru, and with its control of the Homs–Tripolis Gap between the Mediterranean and Upper Mesopotamia, the local rulers were quite powerful.

The pressure of the Hittites, led by Suppiluliuma and his son, Mursilis II, ensured that Amurru was no longer pro-Egyptian. The former ultimately reduced the kingdom of Mitanni to minor status. Amurru then swung to Hatti, while retaining its inherent unity and local independence. It lay across

Seti I advancing against the Hittites. Exterior north wall, west wing of the Hypostyle Hall, Karnak, Thebes. This scene is on the bottom register and shows the situation of the Hittite commander fighting in a chariot with only one additional man, the charioteer. (Courtesy of Peter Brand)

The site of Kadesh

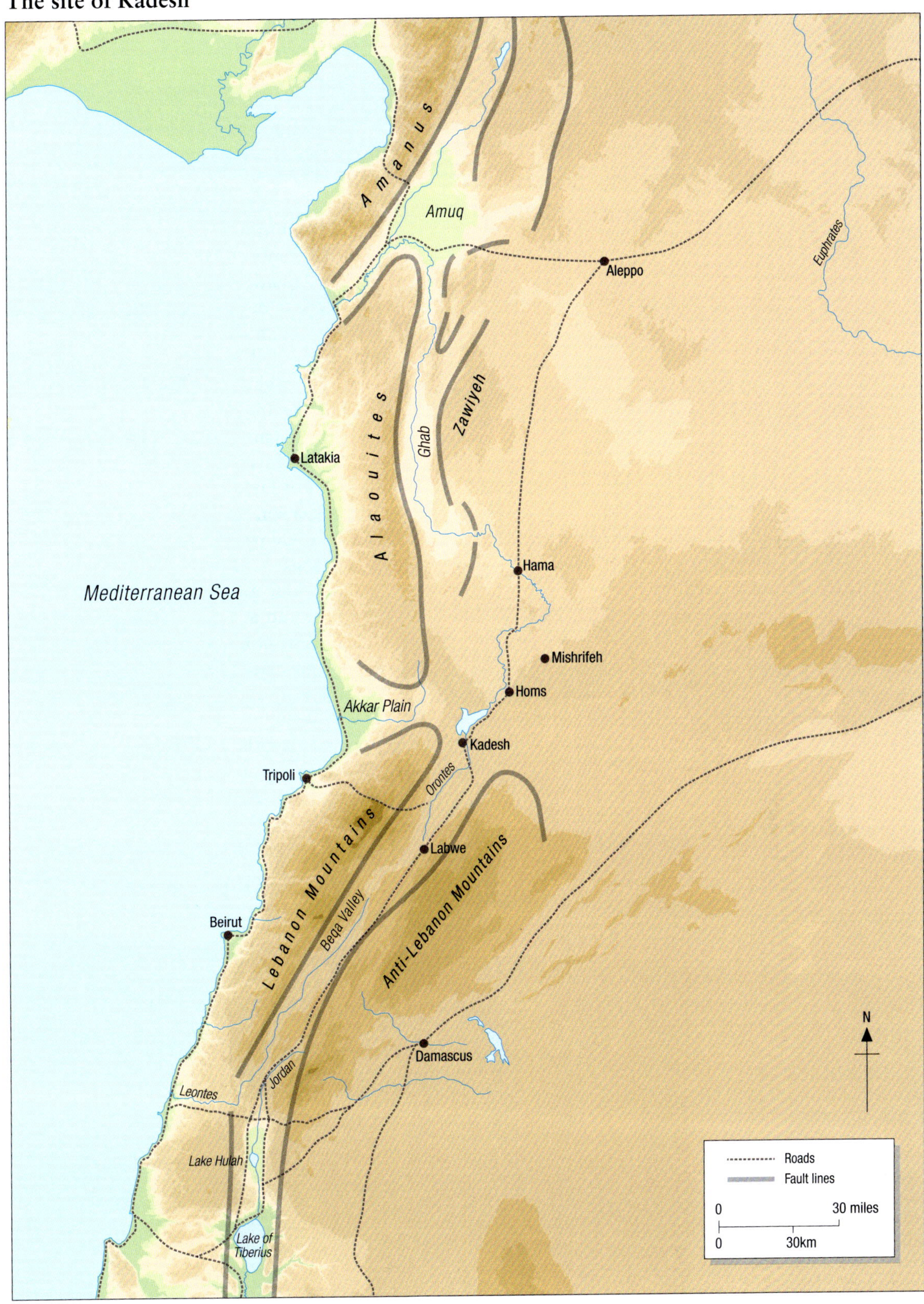

Seti advancing against the city of Kadesh. Exterior west side of the Hypostyle Hall. This scene, on the top register, shows the pharaoh in traditional pose, attacking the enemy with his arrows. (Courtesy of Peter Brand)

the east–west divide south of the Nahr el Kelb River, with the very fertile regions of the Beqa Valley under its domination. South was the Plain of Akkar, which provided extensive grain.

Under Ramesses' father, Seti I, confrontation occurred with the Egyptians moving into Amurru. On the northern wall of the Great Hypostyle Hall at Karnak in Thebes, Seti instituted a pictorial account of his wars. Although the narrative progression is unclear, we see Seti depicted twice in Syria – once against the Hittites and once fighting at Kadesh. This visual account of Seti covers various undated conflicts with Palestinians, Libyans and Sinai marauders, but the one against a Hittite military commander ominously predates the Kadesh encounter of Ramesses. No locality is named. A group marshaller and fan bearer, Mehy, has been added to the top register showing Seti attacking Kadesh.

Seti I, King of Sinai and Lebanon. Exterior north wall, east wing of the Hypostle Hall, lower and middle register. The former depicts the attack on the semi-nomadic Shashu 'Bedouin' in the Sinai close to the city of Gaza. The one above shows a peaceful reception of the pharaoh in Lebanon. (Courtesy of Peter Brand)

Seti crushing the Shashu. Exterior north wall, east wing. This is a detail of the previous plate. One can see the primitive nature of the armament of the enemy. Note their lack of chariots. (Courtesy of Peter Brand)

Mehy's role seems to be a precursor to the role of Ramesses II's chariot driver, Menna, in the account of the Poem (P). Both men are brought into the historical account and belong to one hidden side of Egyptian historical presentations.

The importance of the Hittite scene at the bottom, dated before the Kadesh snapshot, reveals the Egyptian enemy with only two men in a war chariot. Because the Kadesh depictions of Ramesses and the written accounts indicate that the Hittites had three to a chariot, was there a change in the enemy's war vehicles from the reign of Seti to that of Ramesses II, following Richard Beal? (Heavier and larger chariots would be needed.)

The third register shows the fighting between Seti and the potentate of Kadesh. The depiction remains standard, visibly apparent in the location of the enemy under the front legs of Seti's chariot horses, the gesture of peace on the upper ramparts of the metropolis, the flight away from combat in front of a herdsman, as well as the exhaustion of the enemy. Still, the depiction is a reasonable pictorial narrative of a battlefield show of force outside of the local potentate's city.

Here you can see an early four-spoke Asiatic chariot dated to the beginning of Dynasty XVIII (*c.* 1550 BC). Note the location of the axle. This type was introduced into Egypt earlier and changed to the later six-spoked version by the middle of the dynasty. Note the location of the axle, an issue that re-emerges with respect to the Hittite chariots at the Battle of Kadesh. From the tomb of Ahmose, son of Ebana, at El Kab. (Courtesy of W. Vivian Davies)

OPPOSING COMMANDERS

EGYPTIAN

Ramesses II, pharaoh of Egypt (*r.* 1279–1213 BC), was the son of Seti I and the third ruler of Egyptian Dynasty XIX. He had already seen military activity in his fourth regnal year when he reached the Nahr el Kelb in the Lebanon and set up his famous victory stela there. He had previously dealt with incursions of pirates whom the Egyptian sources called Sea Peoples. He defended the Nile Delta from them around his second year of rule. Hence his earlier years already witnessed an inherited military outlook, one that was a necessity owing to the renewal of Egyptian–Hittite hostility in Syria. Furthermore, he was trained from childhood to be a commander-in-chief at an early age, and knew archery and chariotry among other martial arts. All king's sons of the New Kingdom (*c.* 1550–1070 BC) were trained in warfare, but the extant historical records, both written and pictorial, bear witness to Ramesses' intense preoccupation with war.

HITTITE

Muwatallis (*c. r.* 1292–1272 BC), his Hittite opponent, was equally the son of a successful hero, Mursilis II. Although it is assumed that he and Seti I had agreed to a treaty by which he received Kadesh, there is no proof for this. Outside of the battle of Kadesh, Muwatallis is mainly known for moving the Hittite capital south to Tarhuntassa and appointing his brother, Hattusilis (the future Hattusilis III), to rule over the old capital of Hattusa. Identical to his Egyptian opponent, Muwatallis was trained in war from an early age.

HISTORICAL SOURCES

PICTORIAL DATA

One can divide the source material into two separate yet complementary sections. There are the numerous pictorial representations that plaster the walls of the five temples that present the Kadesh battle. They are, from the south going northwards: Abu Simbel (roughly at the second cataract in Nubia), Luxor (in ancient Thebes), Karnak (at Thebes, slightly to the north), the Ramesseum (on the west side of the river, the mortuary temple of the pharaoh) and Abydos (farther north, the shrine of Osiris):

Kadesh version from Abu Simbel. Classic Champollion drawing, which is the first ever rendered, north pillared hall. It is included for historical and comparative reasons. Note his segmentations into scenes. Note the charioteer Menna. (From the New York Public Library, Champollion, *Monuments de l'Égypte et de la Nubia* I, Pl. XVII and XXIX)

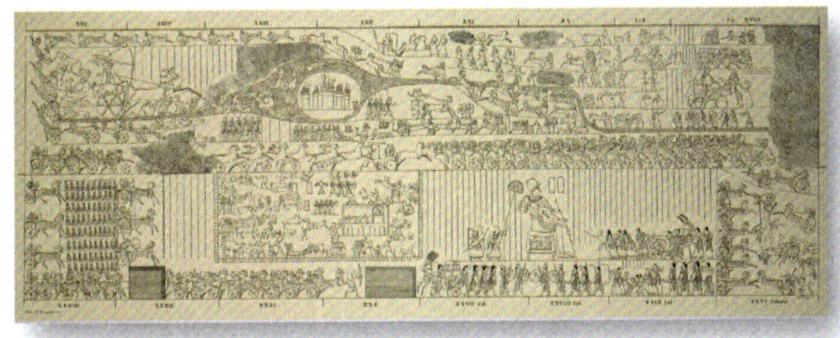

a. Abu Simbel: north interior wall of the pillared hall. There are two registers and one reads from the bottom up. The camp scene (episode one) is depicted in the lower register and the combat above (episode two). Note: the war was in the north and so are these reliefs.

b. Luxor: there are three versions.

L1. The façade with a similar division that is present in Abu Simbel. Both scenes – east battle, west camp – are located quite high and above the two key narrative texts. The shorter Bulletin (B) text is underneath the battle with the Poem, commencing on the west face and crossing over to the east.

L2. The depictions were never carved. Only the Kadesh Poem and Bulletin are present. The location is the exterior east wall (in the front) and south-east walls of the Dynasty XIX colonnade court of Ramesses II.

L3. West exterior walls. At the front, the reliefs and the Poem are placed at the Colonnades of Amunhotep III, and then the linking wall takes you back to the west exterior wall of the Colonnade of Tutankhamun.

c. Karnak: there are two versions.

Kadesh version from Abu Simbel. Rosellini painting of a chariot attack. (From the New York Public Library, *I Monumenti dell'Egitto e della Nubia* III, Pl. CIII)

K1. Four visual episodes exist on the southern side of the Great Hypostyle Hall and they move to the east. First is the clash, then the camp scene and last the post-bellum events. Under the last episode is the Poem.

K2. This is the south approach way on the west wall. From the front at Pylon VIII, the camp starts off the action. Then comes the battle followed by spoils to the king. At the rear (between Pylons IX and X) are the Poem and the Bulletin.

d. Ramesseum: there are two versions.

R1. The rear of the first pylon offers the two major scenes of battle. The north wing shows the camp with the Bulletin.

R2. The north and east walls of the second court orient the viewer to the north, where the camp is, and then the battle looms on the east wall.

e. Abydos: One moves from the exterior west wall to the north wall. The Bulletin is connected to the camp scene. At the end is the Poem.

Detailed depiction of the citadel of Kadesh, Abu Simbel. Troops are considered to be ensconced in the metropolis, but Muwatallis was positioned to the north-east at Kadesh the Old. This depiction is somewhat inaccurate. (From Noblecourt, Donadoni & Edel, *Grand temple d'Abou Simbel: La bataille de Qadech*, Pl. IV)

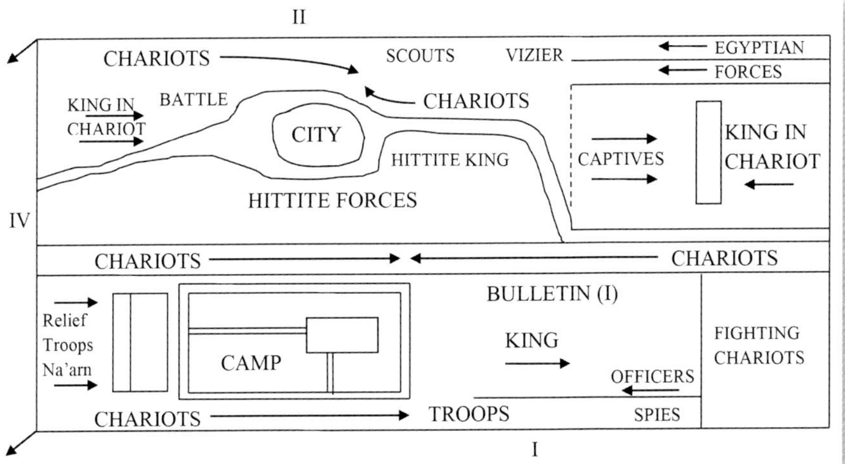

Diagram of Kadesh, Abu Simbel version. The two episodes are neatly separated, with the viewer commencing on the lower level. See the absence of the Poem owing to space constraints. (Original diagram courtesy Brett Heagren; see also Spalinger, *Icons of Power: A Strategy of Reinterpretation*, Fig. 28b)

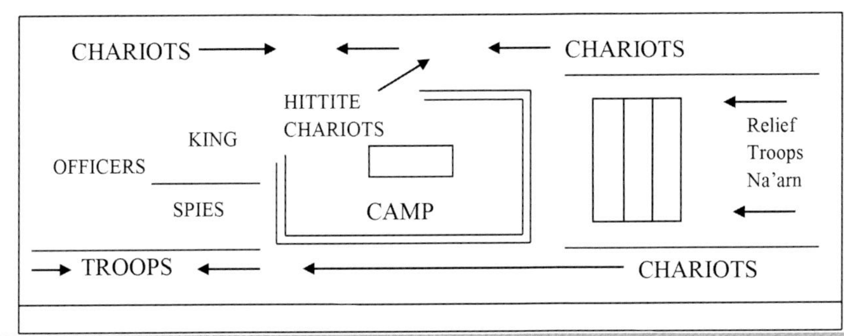

Diagram of Kadesh, L1 in the west wing from Luxor, Thebes. The absence of the Bulletin allowed the artist to provide more details of the king's conference with the spies. (Original diagram courtesy Brett Heagren; see also Spalinger, *Icons of Power*, Fig. 25b)

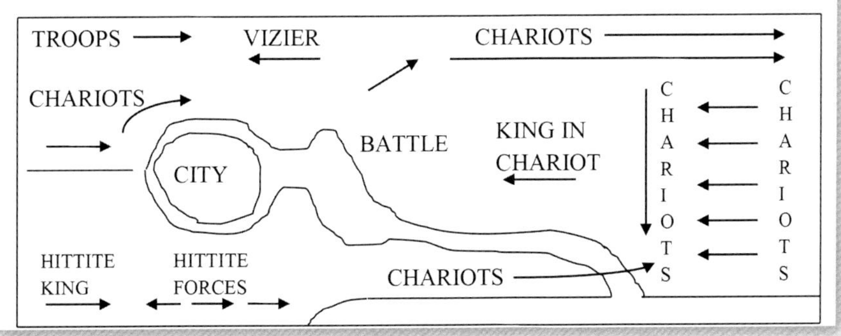

Diagram of Kadesh, east wing. Observe that the Hittite king is placed way down in the relief and far away from Ramesses. (Original diagram courtesy Brett Heagren; see also Spalinger, *Icons of Power*, Fig. 25c)

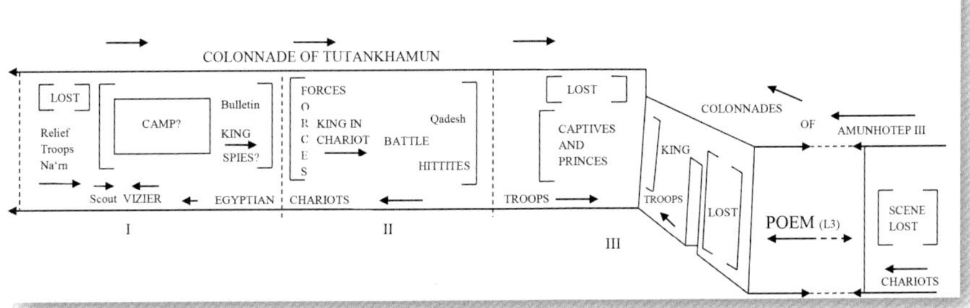

Diagram of Kadesh, L3. See the separate location of the Poem. Episodes 1–3 are shown. (Original diagram courtesy Brett Heagren; see also Spalinger, *Icons of Power*, Fig. 25d)

Diagram of Kadesh, L1. The written accounts face the viewer and the Bulletin is placed next to the Poem and not included in episode 1. (Original diagram courtesy Brett Heagren; see also Spalinger, *Icons of Power*, Fig. 25a)

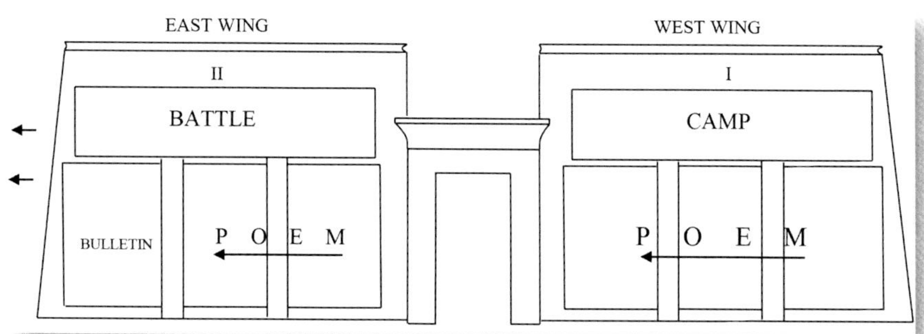

RIGHT AND BELOW
Two additional details of the city of Kadesh. In the Ramesseum relief, teher troops – acting as an elite guard – are located just outside the city's walls. The two versions are L1 and R1. (From Noblecourt, Donadoni & Edel, *Grand temple d'Abou Simbel*, Pl. XXVII)

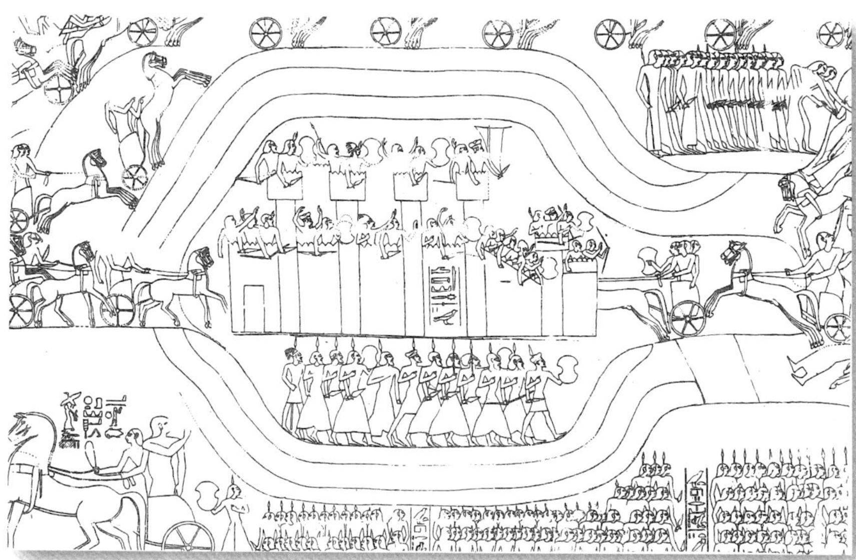

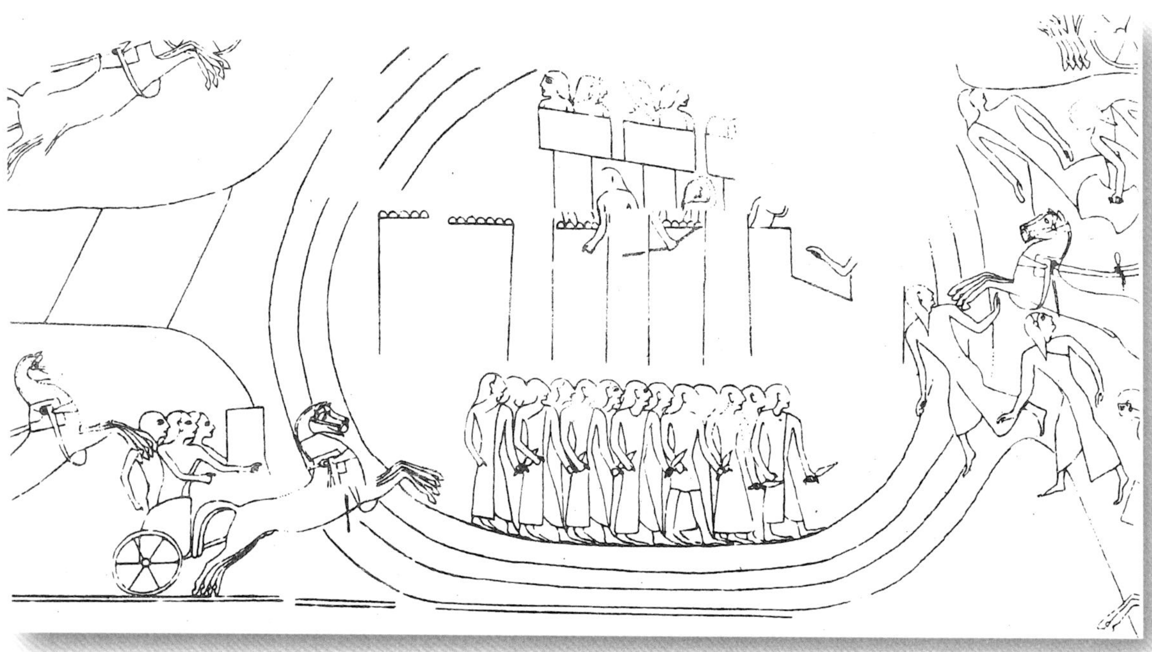

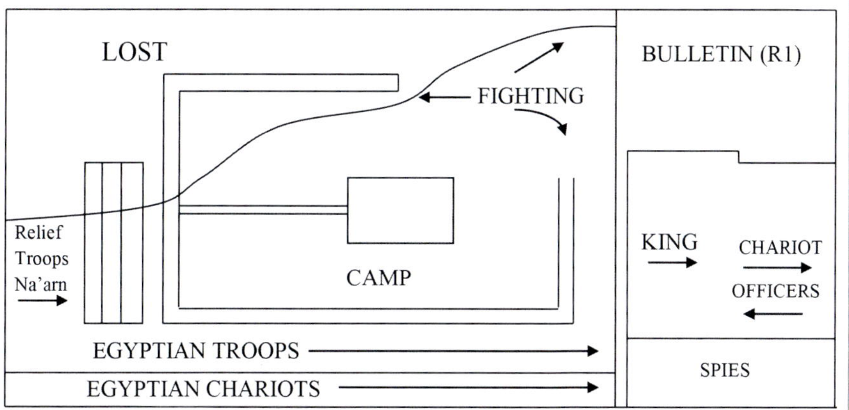

Diagram of Kadesh, R1, rear of the first pylon, north wing. The Bulletin is less integrated into the scene. (Original diagram courtesy Brett Heagren; see also Spalinger, *Icons of Power*, Fig. 27b)

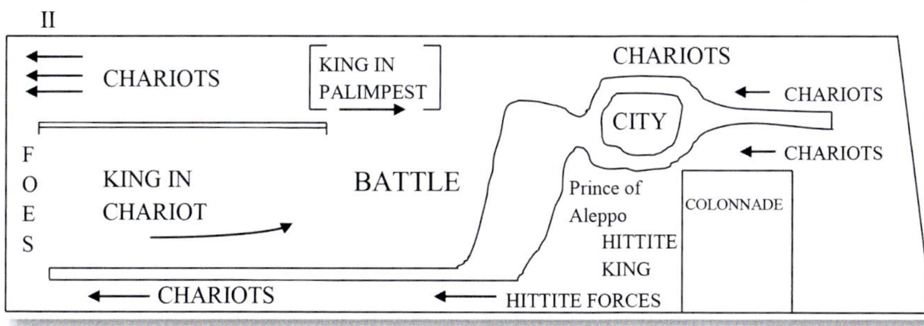

R1, rear of the first pylon, south wing. There was a re-drawing of the scene, which is proven by the palimpsest. (Original diagram courtesy Brett Heagren; see also Spalinger, *Icons of Power*, Fig. 27c)

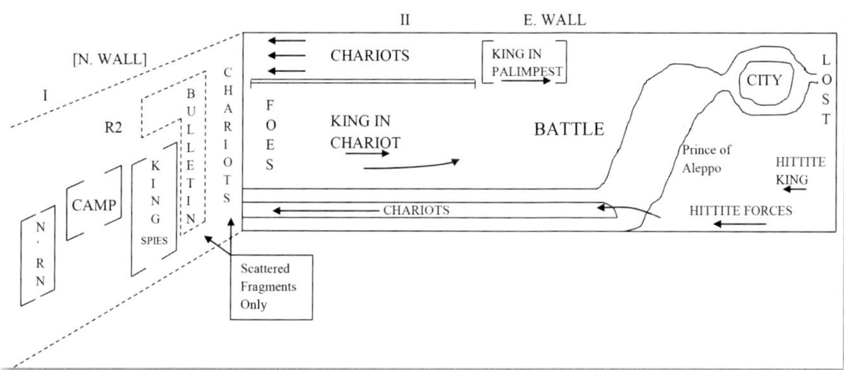

R2, north and east walls in the second court. Note the palimpsest, virtually duplicating R1. (Original diagram courtesy Brett Heagren; see also Spalinger, *Icons of Power*, Fig. 27d)

Kadesh, Abydos, west exterior wall, right side. The advance of the Na'arn, elite Egyptian troops, often assumed to be of foreign origin but this is unclear. This shows the arrangement of an Egyptian cohort as it marches. (From Goelet and Iskander, *Temple of Ramesses II in Abydos, Volume I*, 21)

Abydos, west exterior wall, right side. Again, showing the advance of the Na'arn. (From Goelet and Iskander, *Temple of Ramesses II in Abydos, Volume I*, 20)

Diagram of Kadesh, Abydos. The Poem is at the extreme portion of the latter. We move from the west, where the battle commenced, to the north side, where the battle remained. (Original diagram courtesy Brett Heagren; see also Spalinger, *Icons of Power*, Fig. 28a)

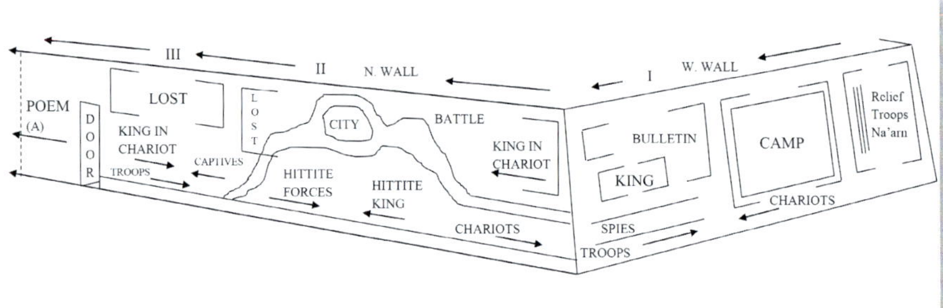

Abydos, north exterior wall, right side. The repulse of the Hittites at the River Orontes. The push of the Hittite chariot onslaught into the river is indicated. Sipazilli, the brother of Muwatallis, is shown deceased. (From Goelet and Iskander, *Temple of Ramesses II in Abydos, Volume I*, 51)

Drawing of the Hittite repulse at the River Orontes. (From Goelet and Iskander, *Temple of Ramesses II in Abydos, Volume I*, 50)

Abydos, north exterior wall, centre, lower section. The reconstructed bivouac of the Hittites at Kadesh the Old. Note the teher warriors and the four-wheeled wagons and oxen for food and fodder. (From Goelet and Iskander, *Temple of Ramesses II in Abydos, Volume I*, 55)

An argument can be made for the 'first edition' being that of Abydos. Abu Simbel, which presents an abbreviated version of the entire scenario, may be the second. At L2, only the Poem and Bulletin were carved; no visual accounts were initiated. The two written accounts of L2 were commenced and finished around the conclusion of the first decade of Ramesses' rule. R1 and L1 were placed at the front of each temple. Their locations tend to indicate a date close to the conclusion of the decoration programmes, but I feel that R2 preceded R1. L3 is quite extensive, and a great amount of exterior free space was used for the Kadesh record. It was probably arranged before L2 and L1. The southern approach way of K2 is straightforward, and one might opt for a date preceding that of K1 (which is a palimpsest). I see a time frame around years 10–15 (at the latest) for K1, with K2 earlier and the time for decoration towards the middle–end of the first decade. In summary, the three incomplete representations of A, K2 and L3 predate R1 and R2, as well as L1 and L2. A date close to the end of the first decade of Ramesses II's reign may be argued for the original layout of L1, but Abu Simbel is difficult to fix temporarily.

Drawing of the reconstructed bivouac. (From Goelet and Iskander, *Temple of Ramesses II in Abydos, Volume I*, 54)

Abydos, north exterior wall, right side. Detail of the enemy. The Syrian allies are at the right and in the middle are the western Anatolian confederates. Note the different shields. (Courtesy of Claude Obsomer)

Abydos, north exterior wall, right side. Detail of the enemy chariot warriors. These are the Hittites. (Courtesy of Claude Obsomer)

Detail of the Syrian chariot warriors. (Courtesy of Claude Obsomer)

Detail of the Anatolian allies. (Courtesy of Claude Obsomer)

THE WRITTEN AND PICTORIAL EVIDENCE COMBINED

The locations of the two lengthy reports provide useful details that reveal their 'independence', partial or complete, from the visually rendered programme of the battle.

a. K1. The Poem is placed in the final position and is located under episode four. It is separate from the reliefs. The Bulletin is next to the camp.
b. K2. The Poem is at the very end after the ninth pylon. The Bulletin is at the right of the camp scene.
c. L1. Underneath episode two (camp) will be found the Poem, whereas the Bulletin is located at the east wing on the left (north) face of the façade of the pylon and above is the battle. Both texts are separate.
d. L2. The pictorial account was never included, probably due to other work being done in the temple. Both lengthy reports are carved side-by-side.
e. L3. The Poem is virtually at the end whereas the Bulletin is located in its regular position at the right of the camp episode.
f. R1. At the rear of the first pylon, the north wing contains the first episode with the Bulletin next to it.
g. R2. In the second court, the Bulletin would have been carved on the north wall and thus linked with the first episode (camp).
h. Abydos. The Bulletin follows the camp scene on the west exterior wall, and the Poem was carved at the very end of the exterior north wall.
i. Abu Simbel. The camp scene in the lower register of the interior north wall contains the Bulletin. There is no Poem due to the lack of space.

The Poem is a lengthy written and epically oriented narrative, whereas the Bulletin, intimately connected to the camp representation, is often considered

K1, Karnak, south-east corner of the exterior south wall of the Great Hypostyle Hall. The Poem begins at the extreme right. The narrative is totally separated from the first two episodes that run to the front. (Courtesy of Peter Brand)

to belong to the 'pictorial record'. The two could be positioned next to each other, separate from the pictorial record. L1 and L2, for example, clearly show this practice. If there were space constraints, the Poem would not be included.

Despite its imprecise dating, the Poem shows unity among all of its exemplars. From the writing of 'Ramesses', one can determine a rough date for the contents of this composition. The spelling of the king's nomen Ramesses, with the double 'ss', is significant and there is actually no difference in writing among any of the exemplars. All of the versions were copied from a soft copy on papyrus written in hieratic.

Abu Simbel presents an abbreviated but lengthier, temporally speaking, visual rendition. I tend to feel that it was set up and carved in the first decade

This is a detail of the beginning column of the Poem. Part of the enemy list may be seen. (Courtesy of Peter Brand)

of Ramesses' reign, after Abydos as well as some of the other versions. The two Ramesseum exemplars generally coincide in design and layout while providing the most pictorial information. They are more detailed than Abu Simbel and L1. R2 shows some later alterations, and so has been dated after R1, which was reinterpreted in the upper right section:

a. R1: Hittite vehicles moving to the left.
b. R2: a combination of footsoldiers, who look Egyptian, and charioteers. But the latter are definitely Hittites.

The L1 version has a major change, as the reengagement of details was artistic in nature. It possesses more information than Abu Simbel and hence is a link between that visual account and those of the Ramesseum. L3, only partly preserved, probably offered a complete version of the conflict. K2 seems to complement it, but K1 provides additional useful data. Abydos provides beautifully raised reliefs suitable for exterior outside walls and presents an orderly progressive development of the battle. We commence on the west wall – suiting the west of Kadesh, where Ramesses was positioned. Then the second episode unfolds around the corner on the north, fitting perfectly the actual combat zone.

The arrangement of the pictorial evidence was logically analyzed by Kenneth Kitchen, who set up a temporal progression. One commences with the camp and then proceeds to the battle. The Bulletin relates to the first episode while the Poem covers the entire narrative scenario. The third and fourth episodes of the visual narrative show the presentation of spoils to the Theban gods.

The Bulletin and Poem are different. The former is more of a narrative than an extended relief addition or a caption. It shapes the basis of the so-called Royal Novel (*Königsnovelle*) 'genre' in which we are placed at a specific locality, with the king as the primal mover who receives news, has a discussion and then acts. Moreover, the Bulletin sets the reader *in media res* and so was, as a rule, placed within the camp scene. We are situated in Asia (the Egyptian Djahy) on a specific day, in a temporarily defined exact month and year, during the king's second campaign of victory.

THE TEXTS OF THE POEM AND THE BULLETIN

The Poem is written in monumental hieroglyphic and presents a modern yet elevated – indeed elite – rendering with specific prefixes and endings omitted. The verbal structure is literary, standing between the Classical phase of Egyptian (Middle Egyptian) and the Ramesside Period's Late Egyptian. The arrangement of the narrative sequences indicates what Jean Winand felt to reflect a Lower Egyptian dialectal preference for such Ramesside (i.e., Dynasties XIX and XX) literary compositions. We are not dealing with the colloquial language or an archaistically oriented '*langage de tradition*'. These lengthy inscriptions were written under the supervision of the highest officials of the day, and were approved by the king at Avaris, the capital. The Poem is an epical chronicle recounting one key past event and provides a literary medium that was distinct from colloquial renditions.

The scenario of the Bulletin is not complicated:

a. Date plus background setting (B 1–7). The narrative uses the war diary of the army at this point.
b. Switch to the arrival of the Shasu enemy scouts (B 8–17).
c. Their information was false (B 18–20).
d. Background to the real situation; Muwatallis' plans (B 21–28).

The Bulletin then narrates the beating of the spies and the conference immediately after, but it does not describe the battle.

e. The king proceeds north (B 29–32). The daybook style is continued.
f. New spies/scouts of Muwatallis are captured; the truth is revealed (B 33–51).
g. The king arranges his conference with the army commanders, with the location of the enemy stated to be 'behind Kadesh the Old'. The high officials denounce the failures of the king's administrators (B 52–71).
h. The vizier is sent south (B 72–74). L1, L3 and Abu Simbel also contain this detail.
i. The attack occurred when Ramesses was still sitting in conference (B 75–76).
j. The army of Pre was in danger (B 77–82).
k. Then the chariots of the enemy surrounded the 'followers' of Ramesses (B 83).
l. Ramesses moves into the fray; factual details cease (B 84–103).
m. The subject changes from the third person to the first (B 104–110). Ramesses pushes the enemy into the Orontes.

The second Hittite attack is ignored because the Bulletin's account fits the scenic presentation of Ramesses defeating his enemies and thrusting them into the river. The somewhat lengthy captions of R 18 and R 19 do the same (R 19).

Kadesh, Abu Simbel, lower register. Detail of the camp scene with the beating of the enemy spies. (Courtesy of Claude Obsomer)

In the Poem, sequential headings separate the temporal events:

a. The king on the march to Kadesh (P 25–40).
b. The situation of the Hittites (P 41–55).
c. In parallel, but as a contrast, the Egyptian march is described with the positions of the divisions stated (P 56–64).
d. Then Muwatallis sends his chariots across the Orontes and smashes through the division of Pre (P 65–74).
e. The pharaoh reacts after hearing the details (P 75–87).

Kadesh, Abu Simbel. Lower register, detail of the innermost section of the Egyptian camp. The attack of the Hittites is clearly represented. (Courtesy of Claude Obsomer)

Then the account also switches from the third to the first person, perfectly suiting the appeal to Amun.

f. Plea to Amun (P 88–120). This provides the deeply held religious sentiment wherein Ramesses pleads and importunes his father god, Amun. This was the most important part of the Poem for Jan Assmann, as it unequivocally presents intense spiritual feeling.
g. Reflections on the battle (P 121–142).
h. Then follows the second development. The Hittite king reacts to the failure and sends additional chariots westwards (P 143–165).

Kadesh, Abu Simbel. Lower register, detail of Ramesses on the throne. The Bulletin surrounds the king. On top is a frieze showing the clash of the two chariot armies. (Courtesy of Claude Obsomer)

Kadesh, Abu Simbel. Upper register, Hittite chariots being annihilated. Note the rear axle on one of the vehicles (enemy has a figure-of-eight shield) and a central axle on another (enemy has a rectangular shield). The cabs are different as well. (Courtesy of Claude Obsomer)

Kadesh, Abu Simbel. Upper register, detail of the Hittite king in a chariot. He looks back at the fighting on the extreme left. The third man with the figure-of-eight shield is about to get into the chariot. (Courtesy of Claude Obsomer)

OPPOSING FORCES

EGYPTIAN

The advance

When Ramesses went out on his fatal campaign to retake Kadesh (year five, month ten, day nine), he had already lost that city to the Hittites. He reacted to Hittite resurgence of military control in Amurru by undertaking a personally led campaign to its heartland. Moreover, the Egyptians had managed a takeover of the kingdom of Amurru to enable them to station the Na'arn contingent of troops at the coast (P 63 and R 19). That country does not appear in the list of Hittite confederates, providing further evidence of its then dependency upon Egypt.

The trajectory followed the expected geographic pattern of using the key routes of western Asia. Ramesses commenced at Avaris, the capital in the eastern Delta of Egypt, and then moved to the departure point of Tjaru/Sile, located at the Sinai–Egyptian border. Then he was in the north: 'When days had passed by his majesty was in Ramesses-mery-Amun, the city which is in the Valley of Cedar.' He proceeded north thorough the Sinai

R1, from the Ramesseum, north wing, first court, rear of first pylon. The Na'arn are located at the lower left and caption R 11 is placed before them. One can see the 'pet lion' brought by the king, as well as the guards at the entrance ways to the bivouac. The horses and pack oxen are separate from their vehicles. (From Wreszinski, *Atlas zur altägyptischen Kulturgeschichte* II, Pl. 92)

Line drawing. (From Wreszinski, *Atlas zur altägyptischen Kulturgeschichte* II, Pl. 92a)

L1, from Luxor, west wing, first pylon, top, including all of episode 1; façade north face. The arrival of the Na'arn is on the right, the camp scenes with attacking Hittite chariots are in the centre, and to the left is the king in discussion with his high officials after hearing of the Hittite onslaught. (From Wreszinski, *Atlas zur altägyptischen Kulturgeschichte* II, Pl. 81)

Line drawing. This copy is very useful because it reveals the first draft of the relief, where Ramesses is seated facing right and the chariots are moving fast above him in the same direction. Note the guards at the entrance way of the camp. (From Wreszinski, *Atlas zur altägyptischen Kulturgeschichte* II, Pl. 82)

to Gaza. From that base, the Egyptian army went inland via Megiddo and up to Syria. This all took place in his fifth regnal year but was preceded by a small campaign one year earlier which ended at the coast of the Lebanon, as his Nahr el Kelb stela indicates. Thus, first the hinterland was avoided, with an inland encounter in Syria to follow. Ramesses' fifth division of troops, the Na'arn, reached Kadesh from the north-west, crossing over from the littoral.

Advance of the Egyptians

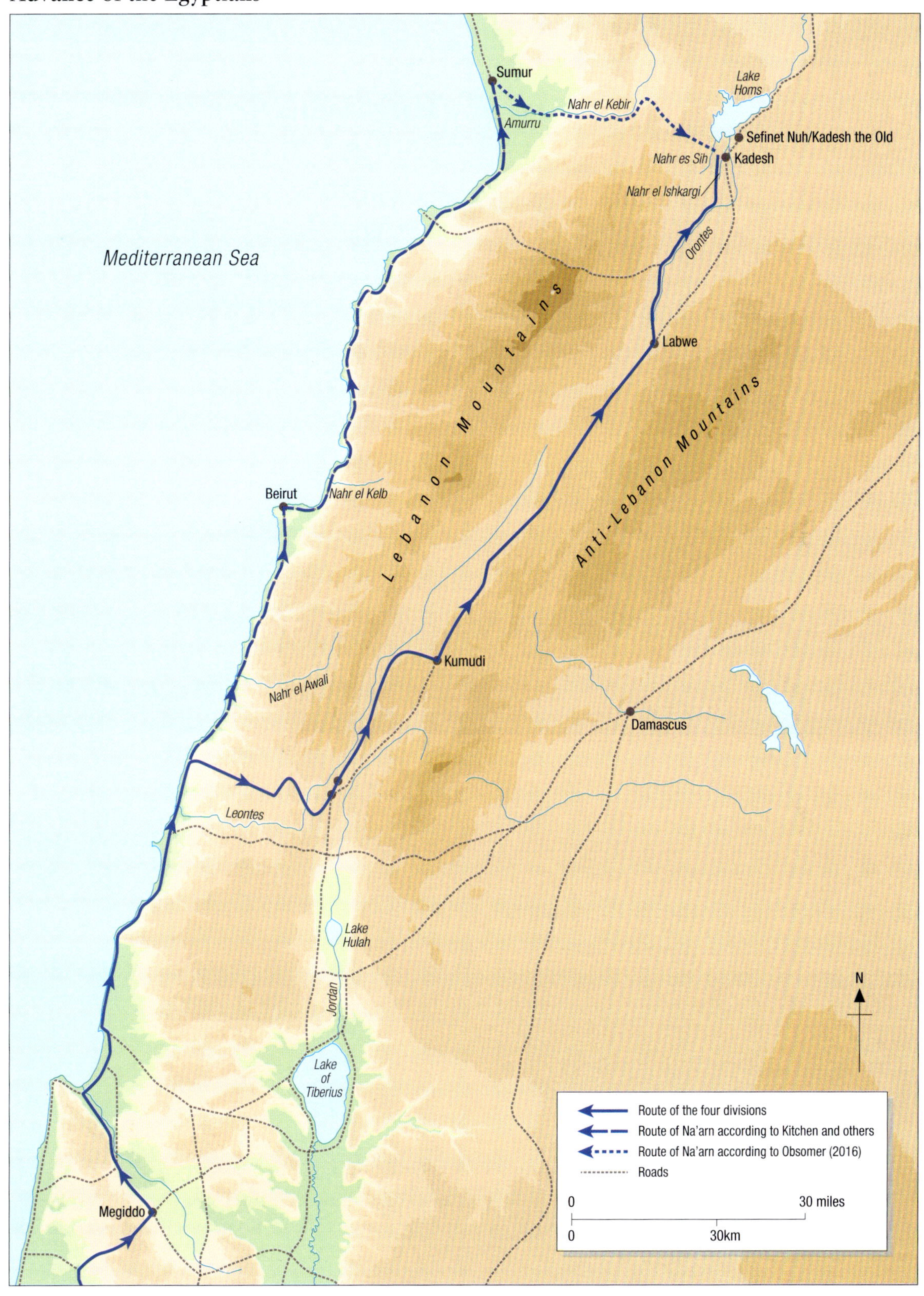

The scheme was to proceed directly to Kadesh. This was a self-evident course of action, with nothing hidden. Ramesses had to defeat a force around the city and then advance further north or east. Kadesh was expected to surrender. Most definitely, the pharaoh did not expect that there would be a great force of opposing troops there, even if he was especially on his guard. He first stopped at Pi-Ramesses, his bastion city in 'the cedars', in east Lebanon, but expected no opposition as this area was under Egyptian control.

Egyptian strategy and tactics

Ramesses ensured that he had brought a large army with him. It comprised, if all men and war materiel were in perfect condition, some 20,000 troops. But we do not know the actual proportions of the chariotry cohorts versus the footsoldiers, who were divided into archers and combat infantry. There were four divisions named after the four major deities of Ramesside Egypt. The first, that of Amun, was led by the king. The other three divisions were those of Pre (the sun god Re), Ptah (Lord of Memphis) and Seth (the war deity of Egypt). Furthermore, a fifth division of elite troops was to traverse southern Syria in an eastward direction from the coast and meet up with the major force at Kadesh. Here is the Poem's specific descriptions of the contingents (P 56–62):

> Now: his majesty was totally alone and with his followers,
> The division of Amun was marched behind him.
> The division of Pre was crossing the ford on the southern vicinity of the town of Shabtuna, at a distance of one iter from the place where his majesty was.
> The division of Ptah was south of the town of Yenoam.
> The division of Seth was marching along the road.

The Poem specifies a period of time before Ramesses reached his future bivouac and was in the process of settling down. One might propose the case

R1, from the Ramesseum, north wing, rear of the first pylon. The king's bivouac, plus the arrival of the enemy. (Courtesy of Claude Obsomer)

Kadesh, Abu Simbel, Great Pillared Hall, north wall, bottom register. This line drawing reveals a combination of short-lived events. The bivouac is interrupted by the enemy chariots. Rows of unharnessed equids, oxen and wheeled vehicles are prominent, as is the pet lion; donkeys are not lined up. (From Noblecourt, Donadoni & Edel, *Grand temple d'Abou Simbel*, Pl. 4)

that the Egyptian monarch had an elite guard close by, 'followers' (Egyptian: *šmsw*), as would be expected. Were they essentially the same as the earlier Middle Kingdom 'guard of the ruler'?

Tactically we are well informed and can see that for any large Egyptian army operating in Syria, a military force separate from the main army progressing north was needed, the Na'arn supplying this effectively. The plan of Ramesses followed the tried and true blueprint for northern military encounters. The Egyptian army when commanded in person by the pharaoh moved along the highways of Asia without much stopping – except, perhaps, for water and some provisioning – until various cities or towns were reached. The army foraged, even though ox-driven carts or wagons brought along the necessary war materiel; donkeys were also used. The Egyptian army settled down near the citadel/fortress/metropolis, as was normal. Logically, as happened with Thutmose III at Megiddo, combat would take place in the early morning of the next day, although this need not have always been the case.

Armed confrontation had to occur because the Egyptian ruler desired the submission of the opposing city – Kadesh in this case – and his opponents refused to surrender. Naturally, the latter situation would often occur, especially when there was no supportive army nearby to assist the metropolis. An expected show of force had to take place soon after the large army of Egyptians arrived. Otherwise, a siege would occur, and this is what occurred at Megiddo under Thutmose III. That pharaoh won the field battle, although his major opponents, including the king of Kadesh, managed to get back into Megiddo. This led to a seven-month investiture.

Therefore, the expected outcomes for both sides allowed the chance of a siege, which would be arduous to Ramesses if it took as long as that of Thutmose. Moreover, there was the Hittite enemy lurking at a distance from Kadesh – or so Ramesses thought – and thus he had to recapture Kadesh as soon as possible. Significantly, the pharaoh made no immediate move upon the city. He reached the camp locality about noon but had to await the arrival of the following three divisions. The time it would take for the final division, that of Seth, to reach Ramesses would be close to the end of the day, allowing no urgency. But his troops were to the west of Kadesh, far away enough, and across a ford as well. His location was excellent.

R2, from the Ramesseum, second court, east wall, episode 2. This shows the 'three men to a chariot' system of the Hittites. The one on the extreme left logically holds the reins, though here the carver has forgotten to include them. In the middle is the shield bearer, and the third is at the extreme right, positioned for archery and javelins. (Courtesy of Peter Brand)

The Egyptians were approximately, indeed conveniently, 1km west of the Nahr Iskargi brook and over 2km from the chariots forces, if we follow Claude Obsomer's reconstruction of the disposition of the enemy's contingents. The account contains the famous reference to the Hittite contingents, 'they being three men on a chariot and being equipped with every weapon of warfare' (P 65–67).

HITTITE

The enemy coalition is defined on more than one occasion in the main narrative account, the so-called Poem and the shorter report, the Bulletin. The commencement of the first account enumerates all the confederates of the Hittite monarch (P 1–6):

a. Naharain. This was the centre of the former independent state of Mitanni in northern Syria. It encompassed the upper regions of the Euphrates and its western outlying metropolises, including Carchemish

L1, Luxor, east wing of the first pylon, top. The city of Kadesh surmounts the Hittite encampment, revealing the fearful enemy king and his warriors at the bottom left. The enemy is depicted within Kadesh and not at Kadesh the Old. (From Wreszinski, *Atlas zur altägyptischen Kulturgeschichte* II, Pl. 87)

Line drawing. This joins to the previous plate. It is a detail of Muwatallis, who is purposely separated from the combat depiction at the upper right (not shown). (From Wreszinski, *Atlas zur altägyptischen Kulturgeschichte* II, Pl. 88)

and Aleppo. Earlier, Naharain was the 'head' of the Palestinian coalition opposed to Thutmose III. It had supported Kadesh.

b. Arzawa. This land was located to the west of Hatti, and its littoral bordered on the eastern Aegean. South-west were the Lukka lands.
c. Pedassa. It is hard to define but it seems to have encompassed a portion of Classical Lycaonia in western Anatolia, between Hatti and Arzawa.
d. Dardany. The land is placed in the Troad region of north-west Anatolia. The name appears in Egyptian sources, but in Hittite texts we read instead Wilusa, Homeric Ilios. In the captions R 79–80, we see the seventh son of Ramesses presenting a Dardanian maryannu to the Theban deities.
e. Masa. This country belonged to the 'Arzawa complex' of states located south of Wilusa (Trojan zone) and somewhat east. Masa was associated with Karkisha and Lukka.
f. Karkisha. Earlier it was located in north-west Asia Minor, yet east of Wilusa and Lukka and north-west from Masa. Its precise location remains problematical.
g. Lukka. This land was east of Karkisha and is roughly identified with Classical Lycia. It was the nucleus of a group that encompassed Masa as well as Karkisha.

The association of Masa, Karkiska, Lukka and Dardany on the Hittite side in the battle of Kadesh obviously does not prove total Hittite control over these countries or ethnic groups.

The orientation then moves from the west (via north–south) to the south-east:

h. Carchemish. We are now in central northern Syria. Hittite affairs in Syria were coordinated and regulated via Carchemish, where the king's agent acted as viceroy.
i. Qode. Although very problematical, Qode's location close to Naharain seems probable. It has to be in northern Syria.
j. Kadesh. The text states 'in the land of Kadesh' and not simply the bare designation.
k. Ugarit. This coastal metropolis in northern Syria was pro-Hittite. The 'governor' of Ugarit was the deputy of the Hittite king and thus extremely important. Note the 'axis' of Hatti–Ugarit–Amurru.
l. Mushanet. The location, while unknown, ought to be in the greater Syrian region.

One moves first to the west and then turns southwards, even if the second list in the Poem poses some difficulties for this interpretation (P 43–47).

R2, from the Ramesseum, second court, east wall, episode 2. These are the teher warriors, presented in a large number to emphasize their importance. They are located to the extreme right (or front) of the east wall and, as in the standard layout, underneath the Orontes and thus also below the city of Kadesh. (Courtesy of Peter Brand)

The enemies recorded by name and rank

The relief captions provide some of the high-ranking Hittite troops who were killed or were drowned in the Orontes. None were from associated states. The mention was due to their prominence. Charioteers in Hittite society were significant, especially the kings' own, and were 'confidential agents', not just middle-ranking soldiers or drivers. The Egyptian charioteers have been likened to 'diplomats'. Those listed are:

a. Sipazzili, brother of the king of Hatti.
b. Targu-nanis, charioteer of the Hittite king.
c. Gilga-Tusu, shield bearer of the king of Hatti; possibly he and the preceding belonged together.
d. Targu-nti-zi[ta]si, troop commander of the people of Qabasu (a state in western Anatolia).
e. Agamu, troop commander of the king of Hatti and part of the core Hittite army; north-west Semitic.
f. Kumaya-ziti, chief of the king's teher warriors. The teher protected Muwatallis. Most did not fight.
g. Harapzili, the king's 'secretary'.
h. Tiya-talli (spelling/name unconfirmed), chief of the bodyguard of the king of Hatti, connected to Muwatallis.
i. Piyas, charioteer of the Hittite king.
j. Sumulatis, charioteer of the king.
k. Labasani, troop commander of Alshe (eastern Anatolia).
l. Hilmu-Zalmu, another brother of Muwatallis.
m. Tudila, chief of the teher warriors.
n. Banuga, charioteer of Hatti.
o. Ziwazis, troop commander from Alshe.
p. Unknown man.
q. The prince of Aleppo, waterlogged after his flight into the Orontes, lived.

Were all of these men present in the second chariot attack or did some of them come with the earlier one? The Hittite contingents also consisted of *pḥrr* (P 84–86). On the Egyptian side, the *pḥrr* were infantry providing support for chariots and infantry. Mercenary Sherden as well as Egyptians could provide this role. They were not heavily armoured, suiting the definition of a 'runner' – light in defensive apparel. However, the translation of 'champion' by Alan Gardiner regarding the Hittites fits better because the sources indicate that the mass of enemy in the first attack was chariot based (Poem, Bulletin, R 19). Hence, the account holds with Gardiner's general translation of 'champions' for *pḥrrw*. Manassa, following Darnell, hypothesized that they served as 'mounted cavalry'. But the difficulty with this new analysis is

Kadesh, Abu Simbel.
The battle – note the spears wounding the horses, thereby supplying evidence of extremely close combat. (Courtesy of Claude Obsomer)

that the reliefs do not offer a clear dichotomy between Hittite and Egyptian chariotry. Lastly, the only time when any of the enemy chariots needed swiftness was after Muwatallis' troops had penetrated Ramesses' second division. As soon as they reached the Egyptian camp, rapidity of movement was considerably less significant. Still, Ramesses' sons were warned to keep clear of the west side of the camp.

Strength in numbers and sizes

One relief caption indicates that Ramesses moved into battle against 2,500 enemy chariots (R 19). He then defeated his opponents, among whom were the brothers of Muwatallis. All were sent headlong into the Orontes. This short account is extremely compressed in comparison to the Poem (P 84). If we argue that the Hittite chariots were roughly of the same size as the Egyptian ones, then:

a. The chariot cabs were around 1m in width.
b. Add about 1m in total for the axle projections.
c. Thus the right–left dimension was *c.* 2m.
d. For the Tutankhamun chariots, which Crouwel analyzed, the data is:
   1) Four chariots were in the antechamber, two of which were 'state chariots' and never were intended for war. The length is 8m and width 3.6m.
   2) Two lighter chariots in the treasury measured 4m by 3.5m.
e. The cab was *c.* 0.5m deep.

We should now turn to the horses. As a rough estimate, the wheel projects out about 50 per cent in length (0.25m) of the cab's platform. Including the horses in front, we must add at least three times that given size. Thus we arrive at 0.25 + 0.5 + 1.5 or 2.25m. I am purposely not including the horses' front legs.

Space in front and back must be included, as well as on the flanks, excluding the chariots in the first rank and the left and right sides. I assume a minimum of 2m when the horses are considered to be in a file. But 2,500 chariots allows one to set a figure of 2.25m + 2m = 4.25m and then × 2,500 = 10,625m (10.6km), a figure just too high. Allowing for a disposition of ten columns, we end up with a length of 1,062.5m. For 20 columns, we arrive at 531.25m, approximately half of a kilometre. By the way, note the width of two columns: 3.5m × 2 = 7m plus a minimum space of 2m, therefore arriving at 9m. That integer is reasonable. Earlier, Thutmose III had captured 924 chariots and worked with 1,900. Muwatallis' first onslaught was therefore 1.3 times larger than the Dynasty XVIII pharaoh's. With 30 columns, the resulting figure is 454m, a reasonable figure.

Thus the number could be accepted, but it is still biased with regard to the Egyptian divisions. Yet the Hittite chariotry of 2,500 vehicles implies 7,500 men, a figure which is considerably greater than a single Egyptian division of 5,000.

Muwatallis had no interest in having his troops stop until they reached the camp of Ramesses, approximately 2km north. Whether Muwatallis perceived that the pharaoh not only knew but also had sent others southwards must remain a moot question. The Egyptian texts only refer to the slicing action through Pre, the enemy presence 'in the middle' of the division and the 'collapse' (*bdš*, which is better than 'discomforted'). The elapse of time between the slash-through enemy and the foe's arrival at the Egyptian camp remains a thorny issue. The Bulletin states that the enemy had hemmed in the 'followers', the *šmsw*, of Ramesses who were at his side. Ramesses then prepared for combat. The pictorial representations combine a bucolic setting with the sudden advance of the Hittites into the encampment.

Ramesses brought with him 20,000 soldiers, including charioteers and auxiliary personnel. Furthermore, an additional division, the Na'arn, must be added. A high limit of 25,000 may be proposed, but this brings an insurmountable problem. On a major campaign, how many chariots per number of soldiers did an ordinary Egyptian army have? Was the ratio 1:10 or higher? This conundrum is further complicated by the role which the fifth division was to fulfil. The Na'arn cohort turned out to provide much-needed support for the beleaguered pharaoh.

The pictorial evidence concerning the Na'arn helps to reconstruct how the army advanced. To quote Brett Heagren: 'A single line of chariots protects the rear of the formation and the flanks, while a number of chariots are also positioned ahead of the main force.' Inside of this formation, the heavy infantry march in columns of 15 men and are armed with either axes or sickle-shaped swords and units of light infantry appear to march in groups of three or four: 'Some of these troops *are armed with quivers and others with javelins* [emphasis added].'

At Abydos, on the exterior west wall, the first inside column has 15 footsoldiers protected by chariots. On the left flank there are five chariots and thus ten men. In addition, there are four closely placed soldiers per chariot (also for archery?). I am not calculating the rear and front series of vehicles and their men. There are at least three rows of marching soldiers – a platoon or squadron – and one can easily claim five columns.

a. Five chariots and thus 10 men = 15 marching infantry in length, and thus 20 men protecting the footsoldiers on both flanks.
b. One chariot front and rear and thus 4 men = one row.
c. Five rows (minimum number) = 75 infantry protected by 20 men connected with the front and rear chariots.
d. Total chariots (minimum number) is 20, thus 40 men.
e. Additionally, tightly placed men per chariot on the flanks but not in the front or at the rear, 4 per chariot.

Thus 40 in total.

For a possible squadron, there would have been at least 155 men and 20 chariots, but this seems small. Nonetheless, we achieve at least a ratio of 155:20 for men versus chariots (*c.* 13 per cent). (If we have four rows, then the ratio is 136 men versus 198 chariots, leading to the same figure, give or take a percentage point.) We can assume the representation is generic, but it allows us to compare the relative sizes of chariot lengths with marching infantry, and therefore conclude that two horses in length as a team are roughly equivalent, when spaced, to three men. The infantry inside of the cohort are larger than those flanking at the sides (the runners). Therefore, the 3:1 ratio could be altered to *c.* 2.5:1. For a division of 5,000 men, we reach a size of *c.* 3 per cent for this depiction, lending scepticism to the details. On the other hand, to organize men for combat there needed to be some type of minimum unit, and this Abydos scene provides confirmation of a sort. The Luxor representation (L3) of the same Na'arn cohort better confirms Heagren's position concerning 15 infantrymen. Furthermore, there are at least seven rows of men. If we allow eight at a minimum, then 8 × 15 = 120 footsoldiers per cohort. Then we add 20 chariots as well, arriving at 120 + 40 or 160 men.

Approximate calculations can be offered based on the height of the exterior wall at Abydos. The Osiride statue is 585cm tall, and for the total dimension of the height we arrive at 715cm as a minimum, following useful calculations by Sameh Iskander. I would say the height of the west wall is 6–7m. Removing one block at the bottom (0.7m) and the Orontes River from the picture allows us around 4.15m for the scenes. We must deduct the height of the advancing chariotry from the top as well. This restricts the space by 0.6m, thereby coming to 3.55m. I would prefer a final band of 3m, which the infantry occupy, somewhat over 0.35m/column. This would resolve the cohort as encompassing nine or ten men, and thus be close to what L1 offers – 10 × 15 is 150 footsoldiers.

The Hittite chariots charged from the east and smashed through the right flank of the protective side of the division of Pre. The first segment that would have been affected was the outside chariotry and their marching compatriots. The last on the left could get away, but the infantry inside would have been caught. Those chariots at the front and rear of the division would be in the best situation because there was no mopping up.

THE CAMPAIGN

THE EGYPTIANS ARRIVE AT KADESH

The Bulletin dramatically commences the record south of Shabtuna, when the Egyptians 'captured' two Shasu spies of the King of Hatti who gave deceptive particulars concerning the whereabouts of the enemy. (Muwatallis was supposed to be in Aleppo.) They must have been waiting for the arrival of the Egyptian divisions. Secrecy was impossible, and it is notable that the encounter occurred just after Ramesses had crossed the ford and before his second division had come into sight. The pharaoh would settle down to the north of the Orontes in a zone bounded by the Nahr Iskargi to the east, the Nahr es Sil to the west and the present Lake Homs to the north. Owing to the false information, Ramesses moved his troops northwards. Muwatallis surely had scouted the terrain to the west of the ford of the Orontes, dispatched spies to ferret out the Egyptian advance and sent a few men to convey false information to the Egyptian monarch. This implies that Muwatallis had placed watchers around the area.

The crisis was yet to be met. After settling down, Egyptian scouts picked up two Hittite scout-spies who informed the pharaoh that the enemy was behind Kadesh the Old, north-east of Kadesh. This is the crucial turning point in the narrative. They were interrogated and riders sent south to the division of Ptah, around Aronama. Then the Hittites struck. The second division of Pre had already crossed the ford 'south of Shabtuna', approximately one Egyptian *iter* (*c.* 10.5km) from the bivouac.

Ramesses then girded himself for battle, despite being hemmed in, and charged against his foe. The remaining section of the Bulletin adds little. The pharaoh repelled the chariots and propelled them back to the Orontes. No additional information is provided as the purpose of the Bulletin is to give a summary of the accompanying scenes by emphasizing the treacherous situation into which Ramesses had fallen.

This account is to be placed in contrast to the Kadesh Poem, epic in orientation and metrically designed. It possesses a narrative outlook but nonetheless does not lose itself in a prose rendition of what happened at Kadesh. Interesting psychological and religious details are presented, especially centring upon the king's pietism. It is a self-standing written heroic saga. The Poem describes the personal relationship between the king and his charioteer, Menna, with a dialogue between Ramesses and the right-hand

First act of the battle

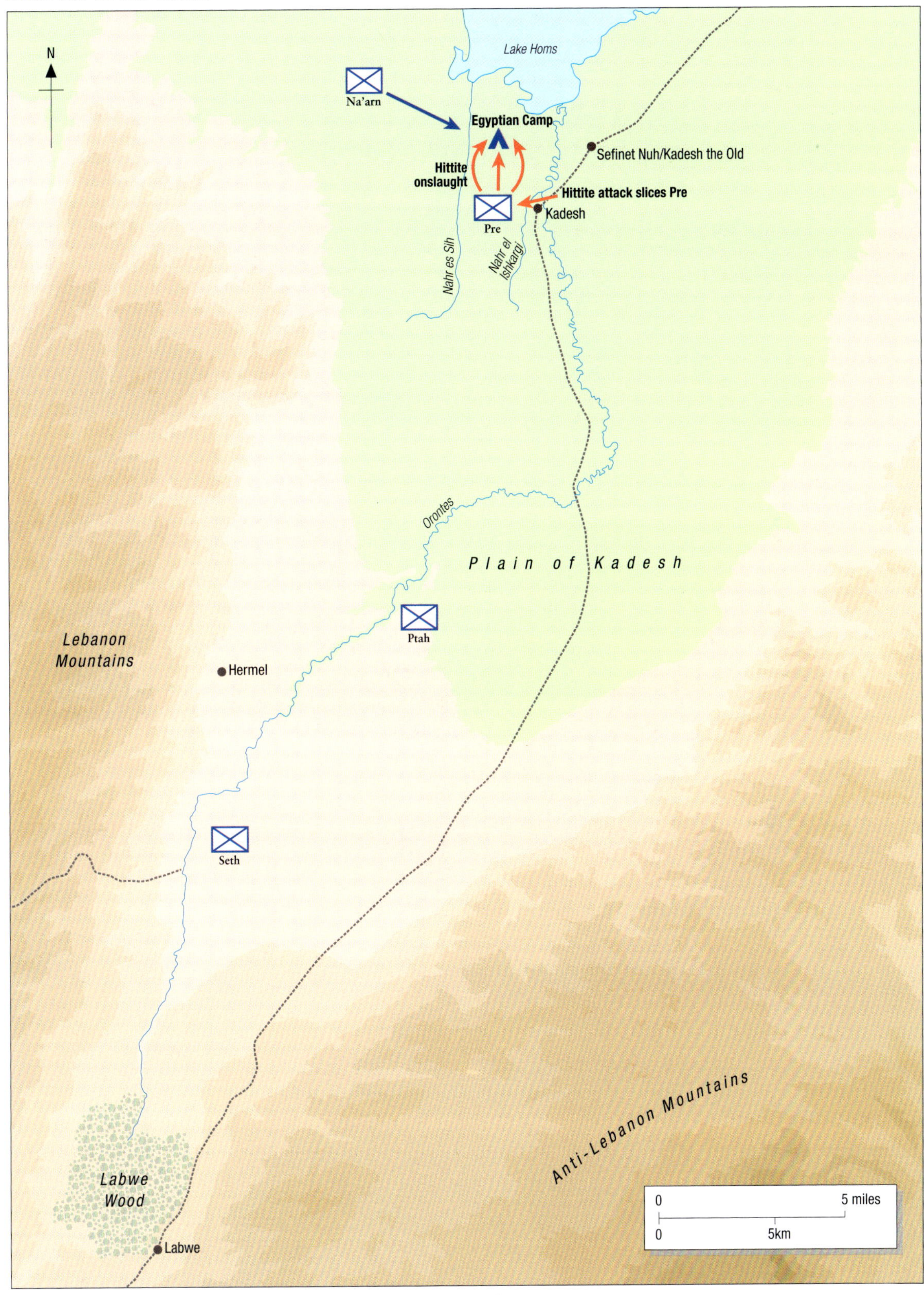

man of the pharaoh fighting in the royal chariot. The fictional aspects of New Kingdom warfare literature, discussed by Colleen Manassa, are linked with the role of Menna, whom Ramesses later signals out at the end of the fighting on day one with his butlers and horse teams.

If the interchange of Menna – who acts cowardly – and Ramesses – who is heroic – forms one aspect of this account, so does the pharaoh's relation to his father-god, Amun. This major dramatic turn of events occurs after the first Hittite chariot attack. Ramesses found himself isolated, and it is this trap that leads to the major spiritual aspect of the Poem. Ramesses was abandoned (P 88–91):

> while there was no army commander, no charioteer,
> no soldier of the army, no shield bearer. My infantry
> and my chariotry were scampering away.

His foreign administrators and officials had already failed to inform him of Muwatallis' whereabouts. Now his soldiers were cowardly. The intention is to describe the solitary nature of the pharaoh, who implored Amun for succour, and this religious characteristic is the key to understanding Ramesses' dependence upon but a few.

The battle would turn out for both sides to be different than expected. Taking the Hittite point of view, Muwatallis had chosen the east side of the Orontes for his encampment and removed himself to the north-east of Kadesh (P 70–71). We can presume that he knew that the Egyptians were moving north-west of the Orontes.

Muwatallis had chosen this location, roughly 2km away, to keep hidden but also to ensure that any dust and noise from the animals (horses) would not be perceived. In the pictorial representations, all of the Egyptian military paraphernalia – horses, oxen, carts, chariots, supplies, donkeys, etc. – are

R1, from the Ramesseum, north wing, rear of the first pylon. Camp and horses. The 'standard' activity of a bivouac is recorded but we may assume that this is artistic licence. (Courtesy of Peter Brand)

R1, lower register centre. Bivouac attack. The Hittite charioteers have been pushed out of their vehicles and then killed. (Courtesy of Peter Brand)

neatly arranged and in order, indicating that Ramesses and his army were initially relaxed. Did Muwatallis just then commence to prepare his thrust while the first division was still moving north?

The temporal development was:

a. Ramesses on his throne awaits information from his scouts.
b. They return with two Hittites and the information is relayed to the pharaoh.
c. The first division was relaxing.
d. Ramesses had time to call together immediately his high officers, and to inform them of the severe danger in which they were.
e. After consultation, the vizier was sent south to hurry along the division south of Shabtuna, which must be the second (B 72–73). We further know that the vizier, plus one royal butler and a scout, hastened south to speed up the third division of Ptah. See R 13 and R 14.
f. No reference is given to the second division. However, since the vizier and the others had apparently reached further south, the Hittites had not crossed the river.

Kadesh, Abu Simbel, Great Pillared Hall, north wall, bottom and top register. Muwatallis once more faces Ramesses but is not linked with the city of Kadesh. This version also contains captions to representations not present elsewhere. (From Noblecourt, Donadoni & Edel, *Grand temple d'Abou Simbel*, Pl. 4)

THE HITTITE STRATEGY

Muwatallis did not plan his attack hours earlier, but with the camp of Ramesses exposed and the convenience of having the second division advancing – and thereby isolated – all fell into place. Because some men sped off without any threat from the east side, this indicates that they passed by the second division. Did Muwatallis now know that the third and fourth divisions were being called into action, remote though they still were? The time to act was now.

a. Claude Obsomer reckoned that the Hittite chariots were at Kadesh because the Poem specifies that Muwatallis had sent his men and his chariots from behind that metropolis (P 67–70).
b. Muwatallis remained at Kadesh the Old, somewhat to the north-east of the city.
c. This implies that the Hittite king had decided only on a chariot attack. But when he ordered this, the Pre had crossed the ford.
d. Therefore Muwatallis decided upon an attack that was purely chariot-based.
e. The Poem further states that there were three men to a chariot (P 68). Was this also made on the spur of the moment or, as argued by most scholars, a new military development?
f. The pictorial evidence has some slight slips by incorrectly providing two men to an enemy chariot. This was a common lapse by the Egyptian artists.
g. It has been proposed by Richard Beal that since Seti I's pictorial representation of his Egyptian–Hittite clash shows only two enemy men to a chariot, a change in the arrangement may have thereafter occurred. However, there is no supporting evidence for the hypothesis.

What was hidden from either was the exact tactical disposition of their opponent's soldiers; and this is where Muwatallis, having previously settled down at Kadesh, had the advantage. Furthermore, he had assembled a coalition of states, all of which were allied to him yet independent. His confederation operated via their princes (*wrw* in the Egyptian record) and thus formed separate military units. But under the commander-in-chief, the inherent fragility of separateness and independence still held. Just like a medieval emperor, Muwatallis could not automatically depend upon his princes for continual support in the event of setbacks.

The three-manned Hittite chariot. The right side has the driver and the left the shield bearer, who protects the former. The 'middle man' is to the rear. Temple of Ramesses II, Abydos. (From Goelet & Iskander, *Temple of Ramesses II in Abydos*, 52)

Muwatallis brought together allies from Asia Minor and northern Syria. All belonged to his empire. The Poem (P 1–6) first presents the Hittite coalition by listing the associated countries at the beginning of the introduction or the heading. They have been listed above from page 30. Naharain, the old Mitanni but now a core dependency, was placed in the second position of importance. The lesser states are located at the end.

A second yet more detailed list is presented at the point when Ramesses began to set up camp to the west of Kadesh (P 30–40). A side element enumerates the pharaoh's opponents, with Naharain heading the list (P 43–47). New are the Gashgaens, inveterate thorns in the side of the Hittites. Arzawa, Masha and Lukka are not infrequently associated with them. They bordered the Black Sea and did not belong to the west. Second, there is Arwanna, still difficult to pinpoint geographically but north and adjacent to the Gashgaens, who were in the Pontic region. To the south-east are Kizzuwatna, Carchemish, Ugarit, Qode, Nukhasse – in central-north Syria, known to the Egyptians since Dynasty XVIII – and finally Mushanet and Kadesh.

There is a third yet short catalogue recorded at the point when the surprise attack of the Hittite chariots is given (P 86): Arzawa, Masa and Pedassa. As Alan Gardiner remarked, 'The texts of the temples here content themselves with naming only three of the foreign lands, but P. Sallier III.2.10 adds seven more.' It is best to conclude that this hieratic copy of later years simply added more of the enemy confederacy without following any specific order.

If the monumental texts are followed, we can argue that at least three lands – Arzawa, Masa and Pedassa – were first involved. Perhaps more significant is the absence of any reference to the key players, Hatti and Naharain. It is very possible that those first three lands were at the front of the Hittite attack. Why else would only they and no other country, especially the Hittite themselves, be mentioned? The Poem adds that those three acted together 'as a unit'. Owing to this, one might suppose that the Hittite contingents were logically divided according to nation/country, yet linked by close geographic or ethnic proximity. The specific words of the narrative describe the thrust of Muwatallis consisting of 2,500 chariots when Ramesses looked behind him (P 83).

TIMING AND TECHNOLOGY

The two passages describing the momentous attack are from the Poem (P 72–73): 'They sliced through the army of Pre in its middle while they marched ... they being unprepared to fight'; and from the Bulletin (B 79–80): 'Then they entered into the middle of the army of his majesty while they were marching and they did not know.'

Both may be compared with the narrator's later reference to the fifth Egyptian division arriving at the base camp. There, the verb 'to slice' is also employed to lay stress upon the remarkable speed by which chariots strike their opponents as well as the surgical nature of their undertaking, as stated in Relief (R 11): 'And the Na'arn sliced through the host of the vile enemy of Hatti while they were entering the camp.'

Far more important for the enemy was the time it would take for them to reach the camp. The general approximation of 2km separating the Pre from the camp seems reasonable. Allowing for a maximum of 35kph, we arrive at six minutes or so. This estimation is too rough, however, as the rapid advance westwards across the Orontes has to be taken into consideration, plus the time spent mauling Pre. I add 2–2.5km more for distance covered from 'south of Kadesh' to the Pre, which comes to eight minutes, plus at least 20 minutes or so for the clash and its immediate repercussions. These very tentative calculations give 34 minutes. This, I feel, is a bare minimum

R2, from the Ramesseum, second court, east wall, episode 2. Close up of the battle. This depiction shows an excellent rendition of a rear-axle Hittite chariot with the men in the cab. Note the figure-of-eight shield. (Courtesy of Claude Obsomer)

figure for the time when Muwatallis sent his chariots westwards and when they would have reached the perimeter of the Egyptian camp. I think that it is just short of the true figure, and I have not contemplated the difficulties south of Kadesh. The Pre division would actually only have around five minutes at best after seeing the enemy charge, and their reaction time was too short to prepare an effective defence.

The reliefs at Abydos, the most well-designed, provide a useful template to compare the enemy chariots with those of the Egyptians. I choose among the temple reliefs this exemplar, unlike Manassa, who preferred Abu Simbel. The axles are all definitely placed in the rear. There is enough space at the very rear of the cab and also in the front to allow the driver ample manoeuvring clearance to handle the two horses. The second man also has room enough to throw a javelin or to use the bow and arrow. Both chariot soldiers are amply located within the carriage.

The development of the rear axle was of particular advantage to the use of the yoke and pole hitched chariot in warfare, an overriding point stressed by Mary Littauer. Some of the occupants' weight was passed on to the draught pole, thereby helping to lower the yoke and thus keep it better in place. This amounted to 9.5kg per horse and transferred 10 per cent of the chariot weight of the vehicle to the horses' shoulders.

The Hittite chariots are somewhat divergent, although there is sometimes a difference among the Hittites, Asiatic and Anatolian allies. As with their shields, the chariots are also different. The axles of all of the enemy chariots – there are more than one type – are definitely in the rear. At the side, the rear portion curves down far more greatly than with that of the Egyptians. The Syrian allies have the rectangular cabs all around. In addition, the three men are squeezed together, almost as if it were unusual for them to operate as a unit. It cannot be ascertained that the lateral area in the cab was smaller than that of the Egyptians. The axle of Muwatallis' chariot at Abu Simbel is not so definitely located at the rear, whereas at Abydos it is.

Given that the mass of three men is greater than the equivalent mass of two men, *mutatis mutandis*, the chariots of Ramesses' antagonists would have been slower, allowing for the same propulsive energy of the horse team, unless the wood was considerably lighter than the Egyptians' wood. Mary Littauer and Joost Crouwel have remarked that the profiles of the cabs are either rectangular or rounded; the Egyptian ones are always rounded somewhat, but not as stark as some of the Hittites'. The sides of all the cabs are filled in.

According to Kim Masters, 'The rear placement of the axle transferred about 10% of the chariot weight to the yoke and shoulders of the horses, making the vehicle lighter but slower than those of the Hittites.' In order to prevent strain on the horses, Masters argues, the work carts by necessity had centrally placed axles. A centrally located axle was better support for three men, but the issue remains whether the heavier Hittite chariots were in fact faster. John Darnell, in his encyclopedia entry 'Kadesh', felt that the enemy employed 'heavy infantry transport vehicles with central axles and three men, carrying infantry weapons'. As a result, their tactics no longer involved using the cab as an archery platform but instead as 'mounted infantry', to use Manassa's phrase.

The inherent difficulty is that all hinges upon modern interpretations of ancient Egyptian pictorial representations. How accurate are the reliefs of the enemy chariots? Manassa was correct in analyzing the bulk of the Hittite chariots as having central axles, but only if we stay with her source, Abu Simbel. The chariot frieze of the Hittite coalition at Abydos presents a different story. I am afraid that no clear answer can be given. Owing to the compressed nature of the reliefs at Abu Simbel, I trust the Abydos exterior war scenes more. One should prefer Abydos owing to its superior artistry. The rows of chariots in the base friezes led to standardization, with the presence of a rear axle expected. If these representations of the manned chariots of Muwatallis indicate a changeover in the Hittite Empire, and not merely in the homeland, then a major transformation would have occurred throughout Asia Minor as well as in north Syria. I am afraid that I do not see this as possible. For the most part, the key difference is between the northern Syrian chariots and the others.

EMOTIONS IN BATTLE

The pharaoh went into the fray as soon as he saw the threat and had understood the danger. Then one of the major themes of the Kadesh Poem emerges suddenly. The king appears to be abandoned. Just as his own administrators and local princes had failed to inform him of the enemy location, his own troops had failed. A refrain commencing in P 88 explicitly identifies those who failed to support their king and scampered away: the high officers, charioteers, footsoldiers and shield bearers fled. None of them had shown loyalty to their ruler.

This hyperbolic statement sets the scene for the king's dramatic self-identity as a solitary figure far away in the heartland of Syria. He turned to his father, Amun, and stated that he always showed loyalty to him. This spiritual encounter occurred when Ramesses implored Amun for help and support. It is unique in Egyptian literature and reflects the pietistic outlook of this era as it hearkens back to a literary model drawn up for Pharaoh Thutmose III. He is described as a desperate man by himself. True, Ramesses is a warrior and pharaoh, but why is he alone? Perhaps the Amun to whom he pleaded was the Amun of the Road statue which the king brought with him, but perhaps not. Yet it is he, Amun, who is more useful than any of the soldiers accompanying him. Unfortunately, no time frame can be presented for this phase of the battle.

R1, the Ramesseum. The king in battle, with slight changes from the original. (From Prisse d'Avennes, *Histoire de l'art égyptien d'après les monuments II*, Pl. 40)

The individual nature of Ramesses' 'call' is so unique and personal as to allow us to accept it as a true reflection of the monarch's feelings. The king was caught. Although Ramesses was always loyal to Amun, his army was not loyal to him. Soldiers fail, but Amun does not. In the middle of all is the solitary hero. There remains the relationship between the living pharaoh and his deity on one side, and in contrast his soldiers' association with their king on the other. It is the concept of loyalty, not deeply held pietism, which drives the royal interpretation. From below, Ramesses lacked staunch devotion, dependability and steadfastness. From above, the god gives to Ramesses his hand – that is, his power – and supports his son in battle from behind.

CHARIOTS IN BATTLE

The vehicles served as mobile platforms for soldiers from which they could throw their javelins and spears, and act as speeding archers. With three men in a chariot, one soldier could pick off other infantry and chariot-based foes with a more effective means of success. Owing to its speed and raised platform, and the presence of two men, a chariot was more effective than an archer on horseback. One can add the lack of stirrups as well as the difficultly of shooting arrows while riding using even a medium-sized bow.

The so-called 'Oriental Chariot Battle' involved intense elite confrontation with men armoured enough to resist the penetrating arrows of the composite bow. Chariots were suitable for defending and protecting the flanks of infantry as well as the rear of a division. The centre pole, which turned sharply, speedily and in a short period of time, was a difficulty. The turn had to be wide: approximately 10m, greater than one chariot length. Various ranks existed in any chariot line, but the interval between each chariot line is impossible to determine. One assumption has been *c.* 300m, but this is based on mounted cavalry of the 19th century. Certainly, the entire Hittite chariot force was composed of more than three lines. As for the advance, the basic trichotomy of pace/walk, trot and gallop (see P 221) was well known. In the Egyptian reliefs, we can see the leisurely pace of the approaching Na'arn. The Hittite onslaught with its galloping horses is present, with the advance troops at a trot. At Abu Simbel, 16 fast racing chariots of the Na'arn cohort attack at a gallop those from Muwatallis' first attack.

At a trot, it has been estimated that chariots pass one another at *c.* 300m, whereas at a gallop that distance is reduced to 100m. Thus you have around 40 seconds to shoot off four arrows at best. I am not referring to the use of javelins (good against the flanks of horses) or spears (likewise suitable in close quarters). The question of turning then comes into play, and here the flanks were in the most advantageous position to avoid direct collision and total confusion, if not destruction. Any system of reserves, placed at the flanks or even in the centre, is unknown. Both sides would play a game in which close combat consisted of arrows and then of spears and swords. After the expected first clash, the formations broke apart and individual combat was the norm. The 'runners', as noted earlier, would have come into their element and assisted their own charioteers in slaughtering the enemy. I suspect that manoeuvring after the initial clash involved circling and swinging around in an oval. Little of this can be reconstructed in phase one of this battle.

The fight must have descended into a close one-upon-one situation in which arrows were

L1, showing face-to-face combat between Hittite and Egyptian chariots. Note the use of archers by the Egyptians. They are depicted as more orderly and tactically superior to the enemy. (Courtesy of Peter Brand)

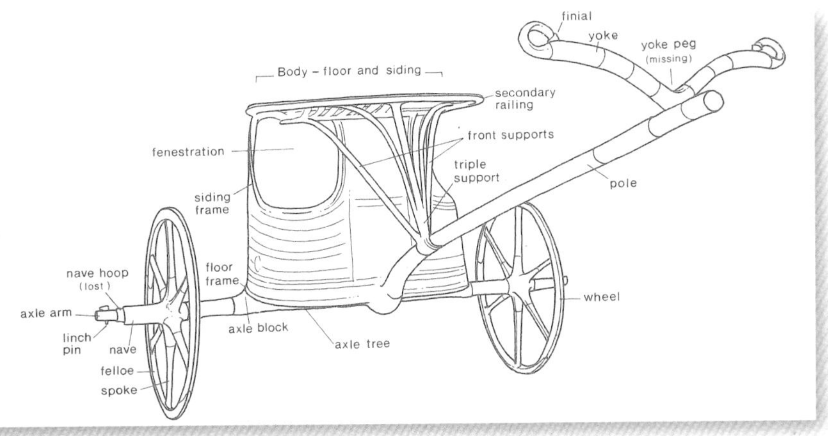

The Egyptian chariot terminology. (From Littauer & Crouwel, *Chariots and Related Equipment from the Tomb of Tutankhamun*, Fig. 1)

discarded, or probably used up, and the remaining spears/swords employed. The aim at this point would be to kill the opposing chariot warrior or disable the driver so that the enemy would have to fight on the ground. It was also an aim to impair the horses as soon as possible. The effects of the third man on the side of the Hittites remain to be explained in more detail. One interpretation is that he acted as a sort of spearman standing next to the charioteer and the driver. Thus, archery could possibly be separated from close combat performed with spears to support the driver from attack. In other words, when close combat was the case, the third man was ideally suited for further defence.

The pictorial evidence reveals that a decided backward shift in the horse's balance allowed for a careful slowing and turning, which equestrians label as 'collection'. The result was that the charioteer could sidestep infantry advancing quite rapidly by manoeuvring around the flanks, thus near the rear of a battalion of footsoldiers. This could have been achieved by the Hittite charioteers at the Egyptian camp during the first onslaught, keeping in mind that Ramesses' first division also possessed numerous chariots. But at this point, the archer may have exchanged his bow for a spear or javelin.

The pictorial war records of Ramesses III (Dynasty XX) show cooperation between the two members of an Egyptian chariot engaging in a direct attack upon enemy Libyans. The drivers hold the shield in their left hand. Next to them, on the right, are the archers. The reins are tied around their hips, after passing through the right hand of the charioteer-driver at their left. Littauer observes that it was the bowman who provided the braking power while the shield bearer supplied directional control on the left. We can speculate that Ramesses' Na'arn may have employed this tactic in launching themselves against the Hittites. Chariots also performed fast flanking movements and

FAR LEFT
The famous chariot of Thutmose IV, right side. The king's chariot wheels have eight spokes. The Asiatic enemies have four-spoked wheels. (From Carter & Newberry, *The Tomb of Thoutmôsis IV*, Pl. X)

FAR RIGHT
Left side of Thutmose IV's chariot. Note the helmet of the enemy chief and the two men in the enemy chariot. (From Carter & Newberry, *The Tomb of Thoutmôsis IV*, Pl. XI)

Wall scene from the tomb of General Urkhaya, Saqqara (early Dynasty XIX). The *c.* 3/4 rear location of the axle is important to signal. Again, see the height of the horses. See O. El-Aguizy in M. Abbas and F. Hoffmann (eds.), *Perspectives on the Ramesside System*, Münster (2023), 62 figure 1. (Courtesy of Peter Brand)

thus could pursue the enemy. Additionally, they also were able to run across the front of an enemy line in order to soften it. But the chariot-upon-chariot encounter witnessed from the very start in the battle of Kadesh did not 'properly fit' these expectations.

According to the Poem, two personal weapons – the hand-held javelins and bows and arrows – were used during the opening minutes of the Hittite attack (P 136–137):

The Tano chariot – a later Dynasty XVIII chariot. (Artist impression by Erno Endenburg/André Veldmeijer from Veldmeijer and Ikram (eds), *Chariots in Ancient Egypt*, 71)

> All of their arms were weak; they were unable to shoot.
> They did not find their courage to seize their javelins.

The combat was reduced to the last stage of an armed vehicular fight. It had to have been very intense and personal, a point which the Poem implies.

One major source, P. Koller, indicates that 80 arrows would be in a quiver, thereby providing ample ammunition for archery. Let us keep in mind that a chariot probably had at least two quivers. In combat, the first role was to move on the infantry line, but this assumes almost no opposing chariotry. Since the flanks of any infantry division would be the most vulnerable, then the chariots could veer to the left and right and move to the rear of the advancing footsoldiers.

The Bulletin sheds a different light on the matter. The Hittites hemmed in the 'followers' of the king who were at his side. At that moment, Ramesses caught sight of the attacking foe and he prepared for battle (B 84). The Poem points out that earlier, the pharaoh had marched 'alone' together with those men (P 56) at the head of the first division of Amun. Later on in the combat, however, they were not as effective as Ramesses wished.

In the Na'arn caption (R 19), the king rose from his throne and entered the melee, 'being alone'. Then he found the 2,500 chariots in four sections 'hemming him on every side'. One assumes that the pictorial evidence shows the enemy chariots attacking the western fringes of the Egyptian position, but that is all. R 19 is significant in detail. It hastens the actions by providing the final splash, so to speak, of the enemy plunging into the Orontes. The second Hittite chariot attack is ignored. In L1, the original bucolic aspect is interrupted to the west. There is hand-to-hand fighting at the home base. Egyptians on foot attack Hittites in chariots and also dispatch one foe. Enemy chariots enter the periphery of the bivouac, move to the upper right and end up facing a cohort of Na'arn chariots proceeding left (west). (See that the artists have rendered two Hittites per chariot.) In the upper portions, additional combat within the perimeter takes place on foot. Again, this occurs within the perimeter and not outside of it. Below are two of Ramesses' sons about to go away in a chariot.

THE NA'ARN AND THE BELEAGUERED CAMP

Upon examining the important Na'arn representation, a division into three army components is present: chariotry on the outside, runners just inside and a core of many footsoldiers. In the Abydos scene, at least one quiver is shown with these runners. They carry no shields. The mass of infantry hold axes and short sickle-shaped swords. They and the runners are not heavily armoured. (L1 and R2 have no runners.)

The Poem describes the entire army of Ramesses (P 56ff.):

a. King alone with his 'followers'; the Amun division marching behind him.
b. The Pre division crossing the ford south of Shabtuna, and in a precarious position. The division was one iter from the camp, *c.* 10.5km, surely based on first-hand information.
c. The army of Ptah was south of the town of Aronama.
d. The fourth formation, the army of Seth, was marching on the road.
e. Last was the fifth division, visually represented in the reliefs and described in caption R 11 and the Poem (P 56–64).

R 11 describes the arrival of the Na'arn:

> The coming of the Na'arn of pharaoh, l.p.h. [life prosperity, health]
> from the land of Amurru.
> And they found that the host of enemies of Hatti had surrounded the
> camp of pharaoh, l,p.h., on its west side, while his majesty was sitting
> alone, without his army, and the host of chariots had hemmed in ...

> his infantry, while the division of Amun in which pharaoh, l.p.h., was had not yet finished making camp,
>
> ...
>
> The Na'arn sliced through the host of the vile enemy of Hatti when they entered into the camp.
> And then the servants of pharaoh/his majesty, l.p.h., killed them.
> They did not allow one among them to escape.

The opening clash took place within the Egyptian bivouac. Various stages of the war narrative are presented in the scene, such as the quiet and relaxed setting, the initial attack, the Egyptian reaction in the camp and finally the Egyptian counter-attack. But the depictions do not provide the timings of the Egyptian reactions. The Bulletin offers more information that earlier, Ramesses was conferring with his officials when the Hittite king surprised him in his chariot thrust. Advance help from the south had already been sought (B 83–84).

In the Poem, a similar report is presented. First, at a gallop, Ramesses enters the mass of Hittites. Thereupon in a second narrative sequence the king went forth 'to look around him', and then found those 2,500 chariots 'hemming him in' (P 80–84). Suddenly, Ramesses discovered the entire Hittite forces were there, *en face* so to speak. This all occurred when he left the camp.

> And on every side of him he found 2,500 chariots in four bodies had surrounded him, no one with him.

And with the subsequent push back:

> He killed all the princes of all foreign lands and all the brothers of the fallen one of Hatti together with his high officials, his infantry, and his chariotry.
> Then he threw them all down headlong, head over faces.
> And then he caused that they tumble one after the other into the water of the Orontes.

The following can be reconstructed from both main sources:

a. King hears of location of Hittites.
b. King has consultation.
c. He arranges advance notice to be sent by horseback to the south.
d. Hittite wave crosses the Orontes.
e. Hittite chariots slice through the division of Pre.
f. That information is relayed to Ramesses.
g. He prepares for battle.
h. King enters the fray at a gallop.

The time that elapsed for these events has been estimated. At least half an hour can be argued for the time it took the Hittite chariots to leave the eastern side of the Orontes, and we presume that they were stationed at Kadesh. A maximum of 45 minutes suffices for the distances travelled, but how long it took them to cut through the division of Pre is a troublesome question. To three-quarters of an hour add at least 15 minutes for the time that the new information was given to the pharaoh and his immediate preparations. But how long did it take Muwatallis to cut through the division of Pre? Considering the rapid enemy charge, the slow Egyptian advance and the avoidance of eliminating the Egyptians, those Hittite chariots ought to have perforated the Pre troops in little time. I can see around 30 minutes plus in total.

The arrival of the Na'arn from the west found the Hittite chariots hemming the camp of the Egyptian king and entering it. The pitching of the camp was not completed, although we may assume an extension of the bivouac was begun to include the additional divisions that were expected. The Na'arn thrust themselves against the newly arrived chariot host. It remains an open question as to who the 'followers' were. Some view them as an elite bodyguard. If so, they would have seen intense combat at the very time that Muwatallis' fast troops came upon them. Why are they not mentioned in the conclusion to the day's fighting, where Ramesses praises the few who have supported him, among whom were the royal butlers?

The relief account R 11 further records a precisely arranged temporal progression:

a. The Na'arn broke through the Hittite chariots that were surrounding the king in his camp.
b. The word used is the same one that the Poem earlier employed when the Hittite chariots 'sliced through' the division of Pre.
c. The reliefs show the same thing. L1 and Abu Simbel depict the camp with Egyptian troops speedily advancing upwards in order to attack the Hittites. The second also provides clearer evidence of footsoldiers in the camp preparing for combat against Hittites.
d. It is stated that the 'servants of His majesty' killed the enemy. No butlers or followers of Ramesses are mentioned.

It is an extraordinarily great coincidence that the Na'arn reached the Egyptian camp at about the same time as did the Hittite chariots. How did this occur? The Egyptian monarch did not send advance scouts or officials to meet them. Thus the Na'arn were very close to the bivouac and needed no urgent pressure. By contrast, the vizier went south, first to encounter the second division of Pre which was, after all, south of Shabtuna, and then further on to hasten the division of Ptah. When Ramesses was already 'under siege', they reached the bivouac. R 11 explicitly records that the camp was not yet completely set up and that the king was still sitting alone. The Na'arn broke into the battle lines of the Hittite chariots as the latter were just entering the Egyptian encampment. They, and the 'servants of his majesty', killed the Hittite charioteer warriors in the camp. One has argued that the first division was so demoralized that it could no longer fight as a unit. This is inaccurate.

The Na'arn are not singled out at the conclusion of the day when Ramesses stops fighting. At that point, he stresses his solitary actions with the two royal chariot teams, Victory-in-Thebes and Mut-is-Content. He additionally refers to his chariot driver, Menna, who played an important personal role in the later proceedings of combat, and the household butlers 'who were at his side'. They alone get commendation. We can surmise that

HITTITES SURPRISE THE EGYPTIANS (PP.50–51)

The Hittites staged an effective breakthrough and Ramesses II is preparing to counter-attack. His chariot troops are speeding out of the camp with some infantry support shown at the perimeter **(1)**. Note that the pharaoh **(2)** is waiting for his chariot driver, Menna. By this time, the fifth division, that of the Na'arn, had reached the Egyptian camp and effectively staunched the enemy threat. Ultimately, all depended now upon the number of chariots on each side and the effectiveness of the pharaoh in providing a courageous counter-thrust to the major threat.

This was the most crucial stage – as it was then that Ramesses, with the help of the Na'arn, effectively pierced through the Hittite chariots and engaged them to the south of the bivouac.

the Hittites reached and entered the camp of Ramesses when he was isolated and surrounded by his trustworthy elite guard. But then the Na'arn pressed their counterblow and Ramesses rode into combat in the field. Yet the Na'arn do not play any further role.

Ramesses was 'hemmed in' on his outer side and could not depend upon them. After all, were they not already racing in full battle gear to the bivouac? This is precisely when the lengthy address of Ramesses to Amun takes place, with the repetitive vituperation regarding his troops caused by the inability of most of the camp soldiers to fight. It was up to Ramesses to reply upon his closely knit group of royal butlers surrounding him, with the Na'arn just arriving.

COMBAT IN THE FIELD: FIRST STAGE

What took place after Ramesses finished imploring his father-god, Amun? None of the written documents help us much and we are forced to examine the pictorial accounts. Let us take the Abu Simbel version as a primary case. To the right of the camp, in the upper corner of the picture, the advancing swift chariots of the relief division of the Na'arn attempted to cut through the camp. Within the Egyptian perimeter, the following are the essential iconographic representations:

a. Egyptian footsoldiers engage with and kill Hittites.
b. One solitary empty enemy chariot may be seen.
c. The combat is not chariot based.
d. Egyptian footsoldiers with sticks hasten to defend their territory.

The enemy had already penetrated the simple palisade of shields surrounding the base. The Na'arn in turn pierced the host of Hittite chariots which had swung upwards, in a north-westerly direction, only to circle around the camp at its west side. They were ideally positioned to face the enemy chariots in the same general zone. As an immediate result, the fighting took place in an enclosed area in which chariots played a less important role and the bloodshed must have descended to man-to-man encounters, especially when the enemy charioteers were caught on the ground or forced to stop. The Na'arn division smashed into those forces in a battlefield manoeuvre that was not practiced at home. In L1, these Egyptian warriors are directing their chariots against the Hittites and what ensued was a mass of chariots versus chariots, with fighting still occurring in the camp. Thus Ramesses was able to prepare for the fray. R 11 ends its narration by stating that the 'servants' of the king killed all encroaching Hittites in the camp. Ramesses was therefore saved.

In the encampment, the chariots could not help their lord because the horses were unharnessed from their vehicles. The chariots were 'stacked up' in rows, and L1 shows three of them behind food bins to the left. Version R2, in contrast, offers at the right a more complex and confused depiction in which Hittite chariots appear to have cut through Egyptian soldiers who were guarding the stockade. In the camp, Ramesses could not depend upon charioteers or the infantry and shield bearers, whom one might argue formed a guard around the camp. Thus, only the butlers remained on foot. But he must have known that the Na'arn were ready at hand.

The key verbs expressing the predicament involve constriction. Ramesses' forces were hemmed in. His expected support from the soldiers of the division of Amun did not come. They scampered away, although what could they do when they were unable to get to the vehicles which were still unharnessed? One can assume that Ramesses prepared himself for combat, mounted his chariot with Menna and pushed himself out of the bivouac, with the full knowledge that chariot support was available from the Na'arn.

The Egyptians, although caught and outnumbered, had at least chariot support from outside. The collision between two chariot cohorts did not involve any infantry and must have thereby resolved itself into hand-to-hand fighting, with charioteer warriors using spears and swords while protecting themselves with shields. If the Hittites were unable to use their javelins (P 137), this may indicate that the combat was of a very close nature and prevented the throwing of those heavy weapons against the Egyptians. Instead, the immediate fighting was sword- and axe-oriented, with the expected crashes of horses ramming one another or with chariots careening off the sides of the file. In the Poem, the pharaoh 'enters' into the host of the enemy, and the number of 2,500 chariots is given. Afterwards, with support, Ramesses fights a second time and the number of enemy vehicles is given again as 2,500. In B 100, infantry accompanied the chariots of Muwatallis. Were these the Hittite 'runners'?

Archery may not have played any role. Yet one sector of episode two in L1 reveals (right side) Egyptian chariots in which the soldiers are already shooting arrows. They are nicely drawn up in a row, and at the bottom immediately to the left are three runners, one of whom is a Sherden. The latter two are killing their opponents. I assume that they are additional

L1, Luxor, detail of episode 2. One can recognize how schematic the depiction of the Egyptian encampment is. (Courtesy of Peter Brand)

contingents from the camp. They must be the remnants of the first division of Amun, regrouped forces.

FROM THE FIRST TO THE SECOND STAGE

At Abu Simbel, the battle scene shows less carnage but connects the king's victory in the field when he forced the Hittite chariots to be pushed back to the Orontes. L1 is slightly different. R2 presents an identical case and in the lower left the chariot archers are also present. All three locate Ramesses in his chariot advancing towards the river. How may we resolve this basic pictorial trope with the written accounts? In the Poem, there are a series of major events, each aimed at a specific purpose:

a. King enters enemy host at a gallop and discovers the 2,500 chariots (P 80–82).
b. Ramesses then finds that he is alone and so calls upon Amun (P 83–91).
c. Address to Amun (P 92–127).
d. Segue into Ramesses fighting alone (P 128–142).

At this point Muwatallis is supposed to have realized that his plans had gone awry and arranged a second chariot attack to take place (P 143–153),

Phase One merges into Phase Two

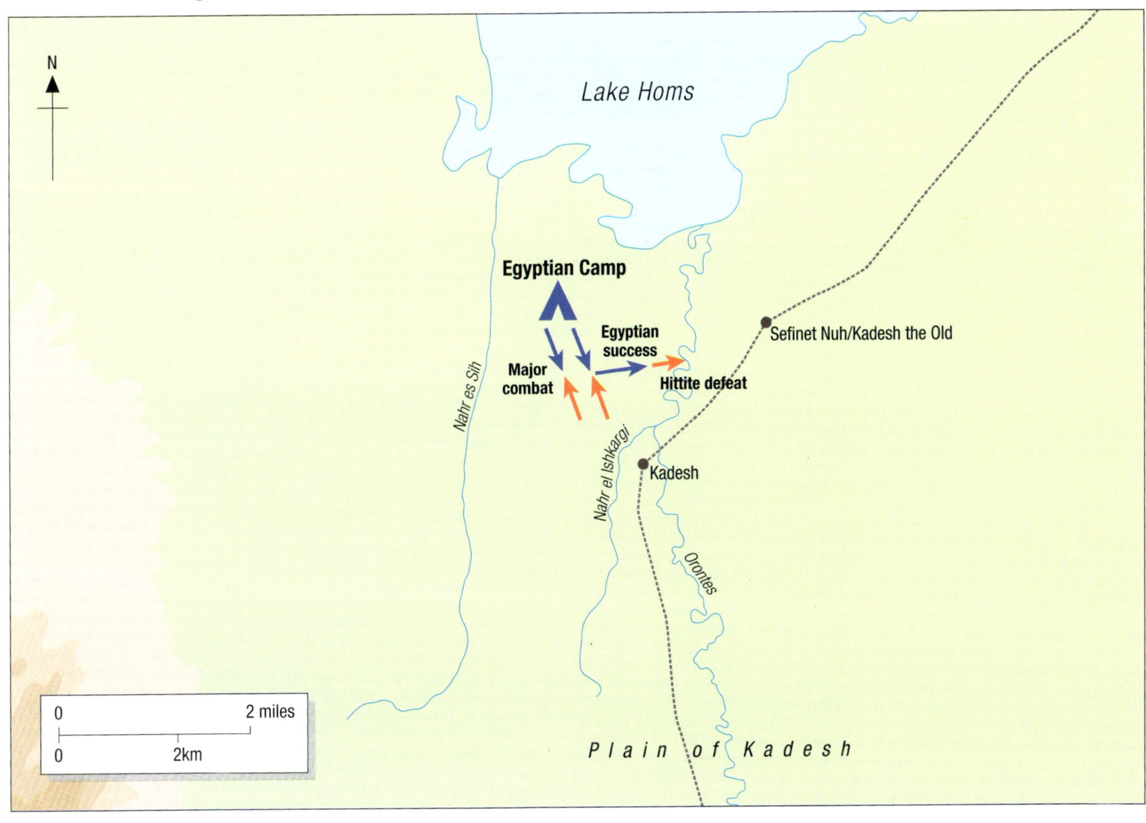

L1, Luxor, detail of episode 2. The king is in discussion, preparing to get ready to enter the enemy's host of chariots. See the royal chariot to the top left. (Courtesy of Peter Brand)

but that sequence moves us far ahead of the actual fighting. This new section opens with the pressures upon Muwatallis:

> Then he caused numerous princes/chiefs to come, each one
> among them with his chariot, and they were prepared with
> all of the weapons of war:
> The prince of Arzawa, the one of Masa, the one of Arwanna,
> the one of Lukka, the one of Dardany, the prince of Carchemish,
> the prince of Karshisha, and the prince of Aleppo,
> the brothers of the one of Hatti were collected in one place;
> and they amounted to 1,000 chariots.

This list reflects the contingents of the second wave. Note that the prince of Aleppo is present, thereby indicating that his presence in the Orontes would have occurred at the close of the second phase of combat. (He was

L1 Luxor. Muwatallis' fear is visually expressed and the caption R 41 reads, 'The vile prince of Hatti, standing, cowering, afraid for his majesty'. The chariot holds only two men, with a third ready to get in. Its axle is at the rear. Muwatallis faces the battle melee *and* Ramesses. (Courtesy of Peter Brand)

pictorially highlighted for humour.) Thus it is reasonable to conclude that the pictorial accounts have combined both Hittite onslaughts into one picture, because the push to the Orontes ended the first-wave attack. Of significant importance is the reference to Muwatallis' brothers, some of whom turn up killed after the fighting ceased.

The opponents in the second wave are categorized as rulers/princes, and not as lands, with the brothers of Muwatallis singled out. The emphasis here is on the great ones, the warrior-heroes of the opposing side, and not on the opposing countries. Among them were the brothers of Muwatallis, the troop commanders of Qabashu and Alshe (R 26 and 33), and the prince of Aleppo, whom we shall refer to more than once in this study (R 40). The other fallen men are all personally connected with the king of the Hittites and perhaps all deceased were from the second phase of the conflict.

The second attack across the Orontes was well designed, having been prepared for some time (P 65–71). For the Hittite ruler, it would have been only a question of when the optimal time would be to attack. Furthermore, Muwatallis appears to have been blessed with an excellent sense of timing – his two charges occurred without meeting any serious opposition. Were his scouts and soldiers hidden amid the swampy plants at the area of the ford of the River Orontes? He appears to have had uncontested control over that area and had enough time to send reinforcements without worrying about Egyptian interference. However, additional chariot soldiers were necessary. To his opponents, Muwatallis was a weak and inactive commander (R 42 and P 65–66):

> The prince, the vile fallen one of Hatti stood
> in the middle of his infantry together with his chariotry;
> his face turned away and his heart distraught.
> He did not come out in order to fight for fear of his
> majesty.

When did this occur? Once more we cannot fix upon any time except to say mid-afternoon. P 164 indicates that during the second Hittite attack, the enemy could not fight him with javelins or bows, and that was 'from afar'. This short remark is useful for analysis as it is the only clear-cut passage that shows the charioteers' reliance on bows and arrows and not on smashing through enemy infantry: 'One cannot take up a bow or a javelin when one sees him come.' The narrative provides a second unexpected commentary on the Hittite weaknesses in battle: 'It was behind him that no one looked, nor did another look around' (P 147). Was this not due to the extremely constricted nature of the chariot fighting? Then came the thrust to the Orontes:

a. P 138: this happened during the first phase of the battle.
b. B 104–105: in the condensed Bulletin it is the final event.
c. R 19: this is the caption to the first episode. There is no reference to two Hittite attacks.
d. R 40: the prince of Aleppo is rescued from drowning. Because he belonged to the second wave, we must separate him from the first attack.

In L1, we see the battle moving to the left with the pharaoh at the right, solitary in his war chariot. In front of him, the Hittite chariots are overthrown

CLASH OF THE CHARIOTS (PP.58–59)

Ramesses is seen in direct combat **(1)**. The clash of chariot versus chariot was a show of strength between the two elite components of the opposing armies. Whereas the Hittite king had not dispatched most of his vehicles, Ramesses was limited by the number he could provide. At best, he had two divisions, and one was partly incapacitated – or still unready – at the camp. This stage of the battle had to have been conducted with speed and intense fighting, which involved attempts to get as close to the chariot opponents as possible. It was, in a sense, a true melee. The horses would have been mauled.

The attempt of Muwatallis to 'catch' Ramesses had failed. In fact, the Egyptian monarch had effectively countered the attack on his camp and moved the conflict away from his base. Ramesses was successful in his defeat of the Hittites. His heroic stand led to their retreat, perhaps headlong eastwards into the Orontes, where some were caught. Others were defeated on the plain. If Ramesses was lacking in numbers, his enemy was likewise limited in combatants, as Muwatallis only sent some of his chariots westwards. He was thus forced to dispatch others.

and driven into the Orontes. The Orontes is artistically split into two portions, isolating the citadel of Kadesh (R 49). Below and to the left, indeed at the farthest position away from the Egyptian pharaoh, will be found the cowardly Muwatallis. He is positioned outside of the fortress-city. Ramesses is on the left side of the river of course, just as Muwatallis is on the right.

At this point, Ramesses speaks to his soldiers, whereas earlier it was only to Amun. This difference is not just a literary conceit. When the new chariot division reached the pharaoh, he continued fighting. In the Bulletin, precise temporal and consecutive narrative elements are fused into one Egyptian counter-attack, yet B 98–99 explicitly mentions the enemy's brothers as well as the princes accompanying them. In the Poem, in the second wave, Muwatallis sends across the Orontes the princes of his allied countries as well as his brothers; in the Bulletin, the first chariot attack of Muwatallis is pushed into the Orontes. It includes the enemy kings, brothers as well as the 'great princes'.

The Bulletin, as befits a smaller and more condensed account, should not be relied upon as much as the well-crafted Poem. From the latter, Obsomer determined that the second wave occurred to the north of the original crossing, which penetrated the division of Pre.

THE SECOND STAGE OF THE BATTLE

The abbreviated Bulletin as well as caption R 19 provide some needed data. Unless Ramesses had pushed far southwards, which is possible but unclear, he probably repelled the Hittite attack on his camp and then thrust the enemy backwards in alignment with that zone of combat. In other words, the first Hittite defeat occurred at roughly the same horizontal zone (latitude) in which the Egyptian camp and Hittite camps were situated. This would allow us to ascertain Muwatallis quickly viewing the failure of his original audacious thrust and to realize on the spot that further chariots were needed. Thus Obsomer's contention can be supported.

But Muwatallis surely had stationed to the west of the Orontes additional soldiers. These men would have kept the entire southern area under their watchful eyes and received information concerning the disposition of the Hittite chariots that were now north of them. Such information could easily be sent back by relay to their ruler. How else was Muwatallis able to determine whether his charge was lagging or had become unsuccessful? But whatever the time of the decision, how could the Egyptian evaluations of the battle have been able to replay the Hittite manoeuvres? To credit Muwatallis with boldness is one thing, but to place his successes upon bare luck is another. Previously he had ascertained the importance of the ford and the need to have many scouts scurrying through the landscape to ensure that knowledge of the disposition of Ramesses' troops was reported back to him as quickly as possible. A weakness on his part may be the supposed lack of knowledge of the Na'arn division. But there, we are further lost in the fog of guesswork.

It is assumed that Muwatallis' second chariot thrust crossed the Orontes close to where the first one did, but Obsomer felt otherwise. The first is an assumption without supporting data, and we would have to add more than 15 minutes to allow the Hittite chariots of phase two to reach Ramesses if he was still near his camp. Here in P 166–204, the main theme is now king and troops, not pharaoh and Amun.

Phase Two

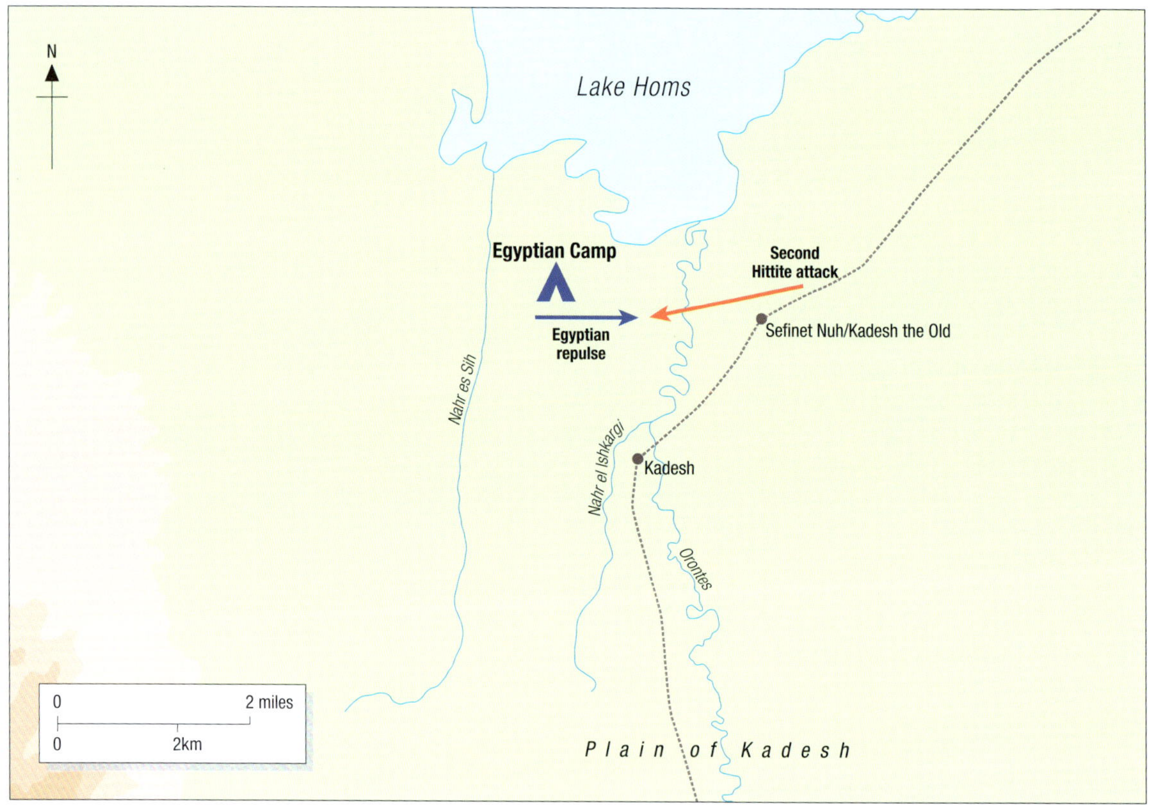

The next portion deals with Ramesses and his charioteer, Menna (P 205–223). For the first and only time, a non-royal personage enters the drama. Menna's role counter-balances the heroic and unflinching stand of his monarch. At the onset, he sees Ramesses 'hemmed' in by a large number of chariots and he reports the threat to his lord.

Phase One	Phase Two
Ramesses is hemmed in at the camp	Muwatallis sends a second host of chariots
	Rhetorical epical interplay
Ramesses enters the fray	Ramesses enters the fray
Ramesses is hemmed in again, but in combat he denounces his own troops for cowardice	Ramesses denounces his own troops once more
Ramesses implores Amun	Ramesses castigates his army
Ramesses states his past beneficial deeds to Amun	Ramesses states his previous support to his soldiers
	Menna enters as a personage
Ramesses finds 2,500 chariots and pushes them to the river	Ramesses enters the enemy for the sixth time

The second narrative segment is abbreviated with respect to the fighting of the king because it switches attention to the emotional turmoil of Menna, thus enhancing further the heroic nature of the Egyptian ruler. The first segment, on the other hand, provides more historically based factors that enable us to reconstruct, at least at the very beginning of the clash, the actual positions and total logistic scenario. Was everything decided in the field after the counter-attack of the Egyptians? Did, in fact, the follow-up of Muwatallis achieve little? One final aspect of contrast is worth mentioning here. The conclusion of phase one is with the thrust to the Orontes. The second part of the day's combat ends with the troops of Ramesses arriving to praise their warrior pharaoh.

It would be fatal to accept the numbers of enemies offered in the Poem. But keep in mind that caption R 19 also provides the figure of 2,500. On another occasion I have listed the four basic types of number-crunching on the part of the ancients when it comes to warfare casualties and prisoners: real, rounded, exaggerated and symbolic figures. There is a fifth, however, and it can be called a 'play figure'. The writer here has purposely offered two impossible integers, rounded and containing a lot of zeros to exaggerate further the victor's great success. Shall we trust the two numbers?

Hans Delbrück's seminal presentation was but one among many attempts to resolve intractable integers obfuscating military accounts. I wrote that it was highly difficult to separate various layers that went into the final numerate redactions. Miscopying, misuse and error explain miscalculation of the slain and captured, but there remains the key psychological motive of falsehood. Did the Egyptians count up the enemy chariots from both forays? That would be impossible. *A fortiori*, did the Egyptians separate the dead Hittites on the first day from the second? Again, I think not.

But the pictorial evidence of the second episode, the battle, offers the actions of the first wave. Let us begin with the eastern exterior side of the First Pylon (L1). The vector of movement is identical to that of the actual event: eastwards. Ramesses, solitary in his chariot, moves east and shoots his arrows against the Hittite enemies.

On the very top of the picture, the wave of Hittite chariots arrives on the scene. The onslaught moves down behind Ramesses until the enemy encounters the Na'arn, also positioned in chariots. There are a lot of Hittites crushed and slaughtered behind the pharaoh. I suspect that these Hittites are those who were tempted to catch the pharaoh and kill him. Thus the visual source tends to duplicate the written declarations of the Poem. Many horses are dying with javelins in their flanks and a few men have been hit by arrows. There are no infantry.

The direction of the Egyptian thrust is to the left or east, so the Hittites fled in their chariots to the River Orontes. This depiction should cover only the clash of the first wave. There is no Menna and we do not witness any second Hittite chariot movement. If we speculate that the size of the Na'arn division was even half of that of the regular cohorts, this means that Ramesses theoretically had at his fingertips around one-and-a-half divisions of men able to repulse the Hittite onslaught. So long as he could extricate himself from the camp, he could rely upon footsoldiers, archers and runners. The Hittite force had slowed down, so by the time Ramesses had regrouped, the clash occurred within a circumscribed area. Speed and agility on wheels meant far less. Two opposed chariot forces collided, with the Egyptians having footsoldiers as additional support.

Muwatallis' bold chance was one that, if successful, would be astounding, but even so a tad too daring. If unsuccessful, as it was, he would lose control of the field but still have enough forces to re-attack the Egyptian army because his third and fourth divisions were absent.

R2, from the Ramesseum, second court, east wall, episode 2. The king moves up to battle. The image of the monarch is a standard one, depicting the war chariot as a mobile platform for archers and for javelin or spear throwing. (Courtesy of Peter Brand)

This is why he sent the second round of chariots as soon as he heard that his gamble had not succeeded. This naturally assumes that he still had free entry and exit at the ford south of the Egyptian bivouac. The master designer of the pictorial account did not add the additional stage in the fighting because the original design provided two necessary snapshots of the king in his camp and in battle.

Was the second wave of chariots lying in wait around the ford, protected from sight by marsh plants and able quickly to cross over the tiny rivulet? Or, instead, did they speed westwards farther to the north? This reconstruction assumes that Muwatallis arranged beforehand his second mobile host in secret. His host was already positioned for crossing, and the second chariot force found the field open to manoeuvre. The third division of Ptah was not yet even in sight; furthermore, no resistance was expected from the shattered division of Pre. Otherwise, as I have tentatively hypothesized, the later thrust westwards could have taken place to the north of the ford, which the first host of Hittite chariots had used.

There were other Hittite lookouts circulating around the western positions of the area and the ford. Muwatallis was remarkably up-to-date concerning the locational dispositions of the first two divisions of his foe's army. This leads to the suspicion that the Hittite king had purposely left men in the area around the ford, highly protected by the gorse, weeds and swampy plants. Hence, those men could have spied out the arrival of Ramesses' first division, its move north and then the second division. The time it took the Amun to reach its base and begin setting up the camp must cover the arrival of the Pre to a zone north of the ford of the Orontes. (An estimate of around 30 minutes minimum appears small.) The Hittite chariot attack sliced through the second division so effectively that they must have been alerted as to the exact position of that cohort. I feel that Muwatallis was very well prepared for Ramesses and that the initial thrust across the river was not a result of chance.

In the same manner, Muwatallis knew when to send further reinforcements into combat. The Poem asserts that he was 'looking' at the camp on the west side (P 143–144). Of course, that would have been impossible unless he left his original encampment at Kadesh the Old. But none of the Egyptian accounts can be trusted regarding any of Muwatallis' battlefield manoeuvres, and I have hypothesized the use of relay men to transmit needed information concerning the fighting. In essence, the Poem emphasizes the personal weakness of Muwatallis, by first avoiding his name but also recording and pictorially revealing his cowardice. He stayed on the west side protected by his teher guard, enormous in number: 37,000 in front of and behind of him (R 43 and R 44; they are to be separated from the teher of R 47). These two numbers are impossible: a) the Egyptians could never have known the totals nor the number of Hittite soldiers, and b) the two figures are astoundingly high and neatly rounded.

The text includes R 43: 'The teher warriors of ... the fighters of the fallen one of Hatti and the teher of Naharain as every warrior/soldier who is before him, 18,000 men' (Abu Simbel version; note the specific locations connected to these soldiers); R 44: 'Other teher warriors who are after him, 19,000 men'; and R 47: 'The teher of the transport wagons of the camp of the fallen one of Hatti.'

They reflect the identical exaggeration that we have already noticed regarding Hittite chariots. If we allow a mere 1.5m in width for an adult male, and include some space between one of the soldiers and the two flanking him (about five English feet), we arrive at 37,000 × 1.5m = 55,500m, a very large number. How did they fit into the city of Kadesh the Old or how big would have been the camp of Muwatallis, considering that we have to add many more men as well as chariots? Then one has to consider the food intake/rations per day. It would have been impossible for such an enormous army to remain in the area for more than a few days with foraging. The costs of living would be very high.

In the same manner, and allowing for 3,500 chariots – roughly 2,000 greater than Thutmose III had at Megiddo – we arrive at three men per chariot, adding 10,500 to the aforementioned 37,000. There would have been 52,500 men. The last figure is, frankly speaking, impossible to imagine. As for the vehicles, 2,500 × 1m width allows 2,500m, or 2.5km, also a very large figure. Still, one must add the space between adjacent chariots as well, and allowing for a maximum of 2m we get approximately 2,500 × 2m or 5,000m/5km, thus arriving at a 7.5km total width; which, hypothesizing ten columns, results in 75km, an integer too great to allow for the advance and attack upon the Egyptian camp. (I allow about 2km for the distance between the army of Pre when attacked, and the bivouac of Ramesses.) Across the River Orontes from Kadesh the Old, there was *c.* 1km or so on the west side. Finally, if we wish to accept the figure of 2,500, the number of chariots on the Egyptian side ought to have been greater than that. As previously noted, at Megiddo, Thutmose III could call in 1,900, considerably less. Thus the figure of 2,500 appears even more exaggerated.

The Egyptian narrative demanded that the enemy size be inflated and the king diminished in power – a common worldwide attitude. The two chariot attacks are considered to be surprises. This attitude is connected to the emotional layout of the epic: Ramesses was bereft of all support. But how did his enemy know of this precise divisional split and, even more, when it was opportune to attack the second group of soldiers? This is why

Obsomer proposed a 'hidden' policy in which the Hittite king would await any pertinent, indeed desired piece of logistic data that would enable him to surprise the Egyptians. Observe that he also placed the follow-up wave of Hittite chariots opposite the Egyptian camp and thus roughly in line with Muwatallis' encampment. For him, the two chariot attacks were executed differently. The advantage of the second assumption is that we can eliminate some factors that would have hindered the Hittite counter-attack:

a. Muwatallis would have been able to perceive from his soldiers at the shore of the Orontes how successful his first assault was going to be and thus react rather quickly.
b. Sending his chariots right across the Orontes close to the eastern zone of the Egyptian camp gave him the added advantage of time (less minutes to elapse) and distance (no northward direction of the chariots needed to be taken).

Muwatallis did not have to worry about the presence of additional Egyptian soldiers from the division of Ptah as they were still south of the ford. Possibly, pictorial episode two may include the presence of this second attack. But the representation of a king in battle is nothing other than the clichéd if striking depiction of the personal combat role of a pharaoh, and the push to the Orontes renders this supposition.

RAMESSES AND PHASE TWO

This stab in the dark begs the question of the equally difficult issue of the latter Hittite onslaught. What was the momentous nature of the final chariot attack? In the second half, we are introduced suddenly to the pharaoh's charioteer. Naturally, Menna's role is to enhance the king's courage and steadfastness. Observe that the Poem provides one specific bit of information in P 220–221: Ramesses (re-)enters the fray at a gallop just as he did on the first occasion back in P 80–81, with almost the exact words employed once more. But the account adds that this was the sixth time. Thus the second phase of battle provides an intriguing and perhaps important remark that concerns the entire development of the first phase. That is to say, in the latter part of the engagement, the king had already moved back into the field on several occasions, but whether all of the preceding five occurrences can be placed to phase two of the combat is unclear. (Actually, we can only identify two earlier cases when Ramesses galloped into the fray.)

Even the brief remarks that the Hittites were unable to use their javelins as well as bows and arrows, presented during the earlier military entanglement, are too vague. During the second round, it may be argued that the collision was quite different. Now the Egyptians could easily see the advance of the new Hittite forces. This implies that the enemy had outriders and men on foot, if not charioteers within visual proximity of the defeat of the first chariot wave. Furthermore, they knew that the second Egyptian division could play no role in the proceedings and that the third had yet to reach the environs of the ford. Therefore, it is plausible that Obsomer's recontraction concerning the later 1,000 chariots is correct, and they sped across the Orontes into the area where Ramesses was already fighting and had the upper hand.

The reliefs of the battle at Abu Simbel might help us because one can argue that the second Hittite chariot force is represented at the top of the depiction. They are, after all, moving rightward and thus against Ramesses but away from the Orontes. That river curves upwards in the scene. If this interpretation is correct, then those Hittite chariots had already reached westwards to engage the pharaoh. If no specific location can be seen in the picture, at least an independent numerous body of antagonists can be determined. Note that those chariots are separate from those whom Ramesses is defeating immediately below. In the latter section, the Egyptian pharaoh has virtually reached the Orontes and is mopping up the final resistance of his opponents. Therefore, the different enemy chariots above might be linked with the second thrust. But frankly, all remains *sub judice*.

A visual distinction is worth signalling. In battle, Ramesses pushed the remaining Hittites from the field and directly into the Orontes. Behind him are the chariots which are said to have deserted him, yet are ready to kill the enemy. Furthermore, even though Ramesses repeats his verbal tirade upon his soldiers at the commencement of the second wave's attack, in all reality one must place that emotion to the events surrounding his earlier dire situation at the camp. Thus the written narrative interposes the monarch's key themes and emotions throughout all stages of the conflict, just as the visual record of episodes one and two do the same.

END OF DAY ONE

According to some of the accounts, the end of the fighting occurred after Ramesses alone had pushed the Hittites back to the river. The Poem, in contrast, continues with the king's achievements until 'the time of evening' (*rwhꜣ*) had occurred. At that vague temporal point, the Poem indicates that Ramesses had specifically overwhelmed Muwatallis' brothers and children on the battlefield, certainly when the second attack was repulsed, and not the first (P 224–230):

> Then when my infantry and my chariotry saw that
> I was like Montu, my sword was powerful,
> Amun, my father, being with me immediately
> turning all of the foreign lands before me into straw.
> Then they betook themselves, one by one, to
> approach the camp at the time of evening [*rwhꜣ*].

The second day's fighting does not matter for the Bulletin and for R 19.

This is the only temporal reference to the time of day in any of the sources. The term '*rwhꜣ*' indicates an undefined, perhaps short period of twilight following the sun's setting and when darkness began. In one contemporary literary account, the word specifies the end of daily work, especially with cultivators. According to Erik Hornung, it designated an amorphous time phase or internal period of the day following the sun's setting. In the Ptolemaic Period, the use refers to the time when the moon and stars could begin to be seen in the sky. In essence, *rwhꜣ* must refer to the period of encroaching darkness and most certainly a temporal interval

CONCLUSION TO THE HITTITE ATTACK (PP.68–69)

At this point, Ramesses had defeated the Hittites south of his camp. The fighting was 'pure' chariot versus chariot. With the necessary assistance of the Na'arn division, the Egyptians repulsed the enemy at the bivouac and pushed directly against the mass of enemy armed vehicles.

Here, we see Ramesses **(1)** chasing the Hittites up to and into the River Orontes **(2)**. This final spree was the icing on the cake. The Egyptians removed their enemy from the west side of the river. It was now up to Muwatallis to send additional forces as Ramesses could not advance eastwards to attack his foe. He must have known of his defeat visually or through scouts operating on foot. The Egyptian record made sure to depict the luckless Hittite prince being rescued on the east bank of the river **(3)**. His waterlogged condition is distinctly prominent in the reliefs.

in which combat would have ceased at least an hour or so earlier. To be sure, the army brought with it a shadow clock in order to determine the time of day. But the Poem regrettably does not mention this nor any other reference to time, as, for example, we find in the war record of Thutmose III at Megiddo.

This issue is significant as it concerns the duration of fighting. Because the Egyptian troops arrived from the south in the evening, after combat has ceased, the time for incipient darkness has to be calculated. With regard to Kadesh, on the ninth day of the third season, as recorded in the written accounts, and considering the Julian date to be on 12 May 1275 BC, we arrive at the following parameters. The calculations are dependent upon Rolf Krauss' research into this matter:

> Nautical dawn began at three hours 43 minutes with civil dawn commencing at four hours 15 minutes. Sunrise was at four hours 42 minutes and sunset at 18 hours 13 minutes.
>
> The end of civil evening twilight was 18 hours 13 minutes. The end of nautical evening twilight was 19 hours 11 minutes. The end of astronomical evening twilight was 19 hours and 45 minutes.

(There were full moon days on 11 and 12 May. The moon set on the day of the battle about 30 minutes after sunrise.)

But if we place Ramesses' accession in 1290 BC, a more probable date, the following results are achieved: nautical dawn began at three hours 39 minutes; civil dawn was at four hours 11 minutes; sunrise was at four hours 38 minutes and sunset at 18 hours 14 minutes. The end of civil dusk was 18 hours 41 minutes; the end of nautical dusk was 19 hours 13 minutes. (The exact full moon occurred on 12 May; on 14 May, the moon rose about 90 minutes after sunset, shedding some light.)

These results allow us to hypothesize additional time spent by the Egyptians in identifying their dead and the enemy casualties. Owing to the renewal of fighting on the morning of the second day, there was no time then for such accounting and recording in the morning. It is most reasonable to assume that the Egyptians took care of their casualties after they had won the two chariot struggles, but later on day two is possible. Acting in an expected and proper fashion, they checked the enemy dead and wounded equally as they did for their own fallen or stricken comrades. Yet after all was concluded on the next day, the names and designations of the elite Hittite allies would have been recorded. At the minimum, the cadavers of the Egyptian men would have been brought back. Although evidence is lacking regarding the treatment of soldiers killed, we assume that they were collected; but the bodies of the enemies were kept separate for later recognisance by Muwatallis' scribes and soldiers.

The ground of western Kadesh was strewn with dead men. The Poem explicitly comments on the situation: 'I had made white the countryside of the land of Kadesh' (P 234). This unusual hyperbolic phrase may indicate that many dead enemies were to be observed everywhere. This could, as I have indicated, have taken place after the end of day one's battlefield success. Some time could have elapsed between those identifications and the sheepish arrival of Ramesses' soldiers. I tend to set the end of active combat around 1600hrs at the latest, followed by scribal identifications and removal of some of the dead. Muwatallis would have supplied his identifications subsequently on day two. Otherwise, all was reckoned at that time.

The fighting of Ramesses in the second wave was, as I have emphasized, a personal victory for the ruler in which his charioteer 'comes to life' as a person. The enemy is not artistically drawn, as was done in the first half of the epic. Nothing historically based may be found in this segment of the battle narrative. Rather, Egyptian soldiers – both segments of the army are once more specified and surely they were from the Ptah and Seth – come to the camp and see their king's physical domination over the Hittites.

The importance of that aspect of astonishment is to provide Ramesses with additional time and space to rebuke his troops. They first praise him in glowing terms, and he in turn admonishes the soldiers. For a third time there is an overt background repertoire offered. In the first, Ramesses had implored Amun and listed his deeds of piety to his god-father. The follow-up personal address by the pharaoh is said to his troops when he, again, was alone during the second chariot attack. The third and final royal declamation is at evening tide. Ramesses refers to himself as saviour and reinforces the ferociously successful role that he has played in combat. We have thus moved from an idealized and distant past to events that occurred just around the corner. It is here that the monarch points out the few who had supported him from the start. They are first of all his two royal chariot teams. Then comes Menna, and he fits perfectly into the narrative as his role is linked to the second phase of combat. Finally, we hear for the first and only time of the 'royal butlers', who were besides him, presumably the men who assisted Ramesses in the camp at the very beginning. The infantry and chariotry, as units, are denigrated as are the high army officials.

The conclusion to the first day of fighting logically came when it was becoming dark. Muwatallis never sent any further cohorts west and Ramesses stopped at the Orontes because he too had no ability to engage the enemy at twilight. Logistically, Ramesses could do little. He had lost many infantry and chariots. Furthermore, he did not know the logistical setup of Muwatallis. The Egyptians, despite the reports given to them at an early stage, never knew just how strong the Hittites were, nor where precisely they were. The only specific information offered was the location of Muwatallis at Kadesh the Old. Nothing is stated concerning the situation at the ford. Similarly, the positioning of the Hittite chariots remains an open question, with some preferring them to be stationed southwards at Kadesh itself.

ASSUMPTIONS AND OPERATIONS OF THE TWO FOES

The layout and intelligence-gathering abilities of Muwatallis were unknown to Ramessess. As he failed in up-to-date military intelligence gathering, he lacked any idea of Muwatallis' logistical arrangements. One can claim that distance prevented him from ascertaining by noise or dust (camp horses and oxen) that the enemy was close by. How long did it take for Ramesses to know that his opponent's chariots were crossing the Orontes, and when did he ascertain that the army of Pre was under severe attack? Remember that he had his own spies around. Nonetheless, the Egyptians were bereft of crucial military awareness.

The two main accounts of the Poem and Bulletin reflect a slanted interpretation of events, just as the sizeable number of enemy chariots signals a hyperbolic rendition. Still, the Bulletin alone mentions Muwatallis being at Kadesh the Old and not at Kadesh, from which the first onslaught of chariots originated. That account presents a more detailed physical layout of the battle as well as the developments. To it one must add the pictorial representations and especially R 11, which supplies significant information with regard to the timing of some of the key events. From these sources we can reconstruct the opening salvos of combat in which Ramesses found himself:

a. The Egyptians were still discussing the dire situation after they had discovered that the enemy was at Kadesh.
b. The conference was proceeding when they also learned that the Hittites had cut through the second division. Some of the troops must have raced north to the camp.
c. The king was hemmed in by the Hittite forces who were also entering the camp.
d. The camp was not yet completely set up.
e. The Na'arn division then sliced through the attacking chariots.
f. The elapsed time would cover around one hour at the maximum, as this did not involve serious resistance on the part of the Egyptians.

Kitchen made some useful approximations as to the number of hours elapsed but he did not know – and neither do we – when Ramesses first settled in. One assumes before or around noon, but all is murky. Given around two hours for the first phase plus one hour maximum for the second, the cessation of fighting would, in essence, have occurred in the mid- to later afternoon, say *c.* 1530hrs. That would allow enough time to fill with the identification of the dead, unless this sad affair was finalized after the combat on day two.

All had occurred owing to the lack of proper intelligence gathering on the part of Ramesses. Independently, the success on the part of Muwatallis relied heavenly upon his own intelligence service. But there is no way that the Egyptians could have later accurately reconstructed the background to these events, much less the number of opponent chariots. Outside of the immediate clashes, such as that against the Pre and the attack on the camp, the narrations are vague through ignorance of what transpired and the desire for a strongly ideologically formed story.

The Poem, Bulletin and the reliefs cannot but present a few personal highlights of what transpired. The push back to the Orontes, for example, is not explained with any telling detail. One has to view the reliefs to gain some type of feeling for the Egyptian success, but even here the visual presentation is a standard or formal one of king in battle. The dispatch of the second wave of Hittite chariots is likewise vaguely reported. Lacking is any temporal setting as well as the quarter in which the subsequent clash of arms took place. Furthermore, in the Poem, the orientation is fixed upon the pharaoh's charioteer and his lord, whereas in the first half, much is spent on Ramesses' cry to Amun.

At any rate, it was impossible to draw up a precise, narratively organized, sequentially arranged and temporally accurate reconstruction of the entire first day's fighting. The epic had to be reconstructed from the first-hand reports of the participants, but needed an accurate report of the momentous actions of the enemy. If we assume, as most do, that the conclusion of the combat took place in the late afternoon, this may indicate that the Egyptians had enough time to make a full record of the enemy killed in battle. But surely this would have been discussed in some way between Ramesses and his foe before all was 'patched up', and it is more reasonable to place such negotiations on day two. I suspect that the total elapsed time for both phases of combat on day one was shorter than most historians have wished. Yet one wonders about Muwatallis' follow-up thrust. Did it occur just when Ramesses was propelling his own forces to the River Orontes, as is claimed? Or was the additional enemy host sent via the ford south of the Egyptian camp, when the way was still clear for additional military pressure? At this point in modern evaluations, note again our lack of specificity, tending to support the more northerly crossing westwards.

A GENERAL EVALUATION OF THE FIRST DAY'S FIGHTING

The outstanding factors of slain soldiers and amount of war materiel seized cannot be evaluated. True, the list of enemy killed included very high-ranking men on the Hittite side. It might appear that some of those men whom we have listed on page 32 belong to the first wave, yet the set evidence is otherwise. We have already observed that the Poem explicitly mentions only three foreign lands that were in battle with Ramesses: Arzawa, Masa and Pedassa. But the account further indicates that those three countries were combined with 'all of the runners' (or champions) of Hatti (P 85–86).

The captions aid us regarding the third episode in the pictorial account. Let us first examine the evidence from Abu Simbel. The third narrative episode is located in the upper register at the extreme right. The king is depicted in his chariot, but his second horse team is identified in R 52 as Mut-is-Content, not his primary one, Victory-in-Thebes. Let us conclude that the latter was more exhausted after fighting or that Mut-is-Content was better suited for a non-combat role. The L3 variant provides the names of three of Ramesses' sons offering homage to their father – Sety, Meryre and Horherwenemef, the 9th, 11th and 12th male offspring of Ramesses, respectively. His first and second sons are not named. Were these relegated later to a non-combat role of official trophy presenters? In the later presentation scenes, Ramesses and his sons offer up the captives to the Theban triad of Amun, Mut and Khonsu. There are the *chiefs* of foreign lands whom Muwatallis sent in the second wave (R 64–66): Carchemish, Arwanna, Dardany, Pedassa, Karkisha, Masa and Lukka. But caption R 62 ought to prove that an official reception event occurred after the victories on day one. Note that living Hittites are brought into the purview of Ramesses. Horses, chariots and weapons, plus cut-off hands, are briefly noted and shown to the onlooker.

Added is the specific indication of the fate of various leading Hittites and their allies. From the second wave are chiefs who led the chariot onslaught.

Those countries in the Poem (P 149–152) can be placed side by side with those taken home and presented to the gods of Thebes (R 64–65):

Poem	**Captions**
Arzawa	Arzawa
Masa	Masa
Arwanna	Arwanna
Lukka	Lukka
Dardany	Dardany
	Pedassa
Carchemish	Carchemish
Karkisha	Karkisha
	Aleppo
	Muwatallis' brothers

The prince of Aleppo is not mentioned in these reliefs because he was rescued on the other side of the Orontes (R 40). Moreover, none of the brothers of the Hittite king turned up in Thebes. We can assume that some may have survived, even though R 23 and R 34 reveal that two were killed. Incidentally, their presence among other fallen comrades indicates that the battlefield list of everyone pronounced dead included both waves of the Hittite attack, as is to be expected.

An additional point may now be presented. In the first wave, Arzawa, Masa and Pedassa are mentioned (P 86). In the captions, the chief of the last country turns up alive, but also present are the princes of Arzawa and Masa, both of whom ought to be included in the second wave because the Poem specifically designates only the chiefs of those lands. With regard to the first phase, only countries are noted.

We can also examine the additional captives which Ramesses' 12 sons offered up to Amun et al. in Karnak. Only version K1 presents:

a. Maryannu warriors of Naharain, Aleppo, the Gashgaens, then Alshe, Ugarit and Nukhasse (together) and Dardanya. (In the cuneiform Armarna Letters, mainly dated to the heretic pharaoh Akhenaton, we hear of Gashga-men transported to Egypt.) They were probably charioteers.
b. Sons of the princes of Hatti (not Muwatallis' offspring), and Masa and Lukka together.
c. Footsoldiers/infantry of Carchemish and Ugarit.

Note the very limited number of ordinary soldiers because the presentation scenes include the important skilled enemies. The others would have gone into the workhouses of the temples of Egypt. This post-bellum captive and booty offering, originally an age-old one of ritual decapitation or slaughter, emphasize the importance of these men. Note that the countries associated with the royal sons descend in importance, as do the male offspring.

R 53–55 present three of Ramesses' sons who were not in the uppermost echelon of birth order. We can thus assume that all of the first 12 were at this ceremony. Merenptah's name was added later (R 89). Aside from Menna, a fearful soldier by the name of Nakhtamun spoke to Ramesses (R 22).

This original caption surely stated the army's need for support from the mighty Ramesses. As remarked upon earlier, only the second court of the Ramesseum contains, as this shows, additional written details.

A second relief caption, R 9, has been recently reinterpreted by Peter Brand to indicate that the king's mother, Tuya, was present. In an earlier translation by Sir Alan Gardiner, the name of Mutnofre was given, a personage of whom we know nothing. Subsequently, a better rendition by Kitchen improved the interpretation. These two independent and differing translations, in conjunction with Brand's new analysis, are:

a. Gardiner: 'The coming of Pharaoh's fan-bearer to [say] the king's children together with those(?) of Mutnofre.'
b. Kitchen: 'The arrival of the Fan-bearer of Pharaoh, l,p.h., to tell the Royal Children and the [...]s of the God's Mother.'
c. Brand: 'Arrival of the fan-bearer of Pharaoh, life, prosperity, health, to tell the royal children (mesu-nesu) and the [servants(?)] of the God's [Moth]er.'

We are focused upon the possible presence of Ramesses' mother, Tuya, in the camp. The king's fanbearer reported to Ramesses' children and the officials associated with the God's Mother (Ramesses' mother) to avoid the west side of the camp as the fighting was fierce there. Hence, the king's mother was present at the battle. But the older copy of Richard Lepsius indicates that only some unnamed officials associated with her at home were present in the bivouac.

Other men who are listed only by title include the vizier (as expected), the king's fanbearers (one of whom is seen scampering away in his chariot), the aforementioned Egyptian scouts, the king's butlers (one of whom was dispatched to the south to the division of Ptah per R 13), the 'followers', the 'servants' and additional butlers who appear at the end. We can sidestep the references by Ramesses concerning his high officials, charioteers, infantry and the like.

All of the extant names and designations of the enemy dead, as surveyed on an earlier occasion, are associated with Muwatallis. The labels also emphasize the teher warriors who acted as a private guard surrounding their monarch. In the description of the prisoners brought to Amun, Mut and Khonsu, the elite maryannu soldiers hold the foremost position. It may be

Kadesh, Abu Simbel, Great Pillared Hall, north wall, top. A detail from the final events of the battle on day one. The prisoners are being assembled and the dead counted by the cut-off hands. (Noblecourt, Donadoni & Edel, *Grand temple d'Abou Simbel*, Pl. IV)

worthwhile to signal Ramesses' famous fourth son, Khaemwaset, with his prisoners who are 'sons of the princes of the Hatti lands' (R 72). Near the end of the 12-man list are troops of Masa and Lukka, western lands, and finally footsoldiers (or infantry) from cities such as Ugarit and Carchemish (R 86 and R 90). The final men may prove that part of Muwatallis' forces included infantry, a sidelight that none of the main two texts indicate to have been the case.

Is it possible to allocate some of the dead and the captives presented in Thebes to either of the two phases of battle? Following the charts listed above, I feel that a major group can be placed in the second wave but that those associated with the king of Hatti more likely belong to the opening salvo of the enemy. This conclusion can be supported by R 40 as the prince of Aleppo most assuredly got caught in the Orontes, and fortunately for him, was rescued. Observe the 'secretary' of Muwatallis in addition to the chief of his bodyguard (R 29 and 30).

At the end of day one, the following parameters appear to place the combat into a tentative 'on-hold' situation, one that both antagonists had to face the following morning:

a. The Egyptians removed their Hittite opponents from the field.
b. Two of their divisions never engaged the enemy.
c. Their arrival at base camp was at twilight.
d. Muwatallis was not dislodged. He remained in possession of the east side of the Orontes, including Kadesh.
e. It is difficult to determine when the Egyptians totalled up the dead and listed the key enemies who had been slaughtered. The first day would imply a time near evening twilight, and thus day two is more probable.
f. If only due to the dead, both sides had to communicate in some way; but they probably dealt with matters on the following day.

The official viewing included the piles of cut-off hands, a scene which would fit the very end of the battle. R 59 notes:

> The total of these foreigners whom his majesty smote,
> when he was alone: Hands, corpses – total – horses,
> chariots, bows, and all the weapons of war.

Captions R 60 and 61 add a little to this assemblage, with the latter referring to Hatti as well as Naharain. R 62 conveniently supplements the prior two captions with the remarks offered at the official ceremony of presentation and celebration:

> ... when his majesty commanded all of the leaders of his
> army [the Abydos variant has: his infantry, his chariotry,
> and his (high) officials] saying: 'Bring to me the captives
> of my own booty.'

Thus in front of the generals, colonels, etc., Ramesses oversaw the living captives. The scene is designated as the third one by Kitchen. The two visual sources are K2 and Abydos. The latter places this episode right after the

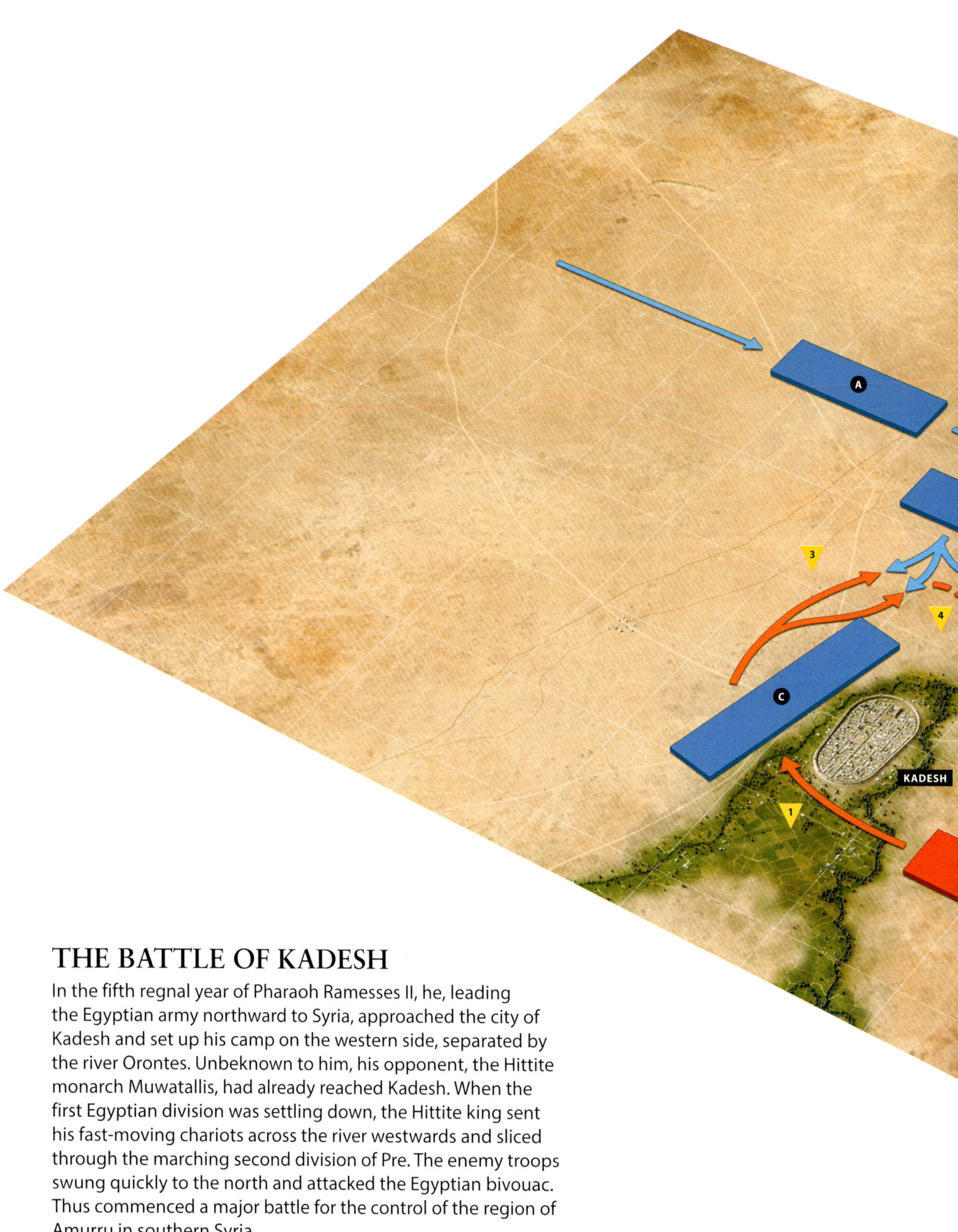

THE BATTLE OF KADESH

In the fifth regnal year of Pharaoh Ramesses II, he, leading the Egyptian army northward to Syria, approached the city of Kadesh and set up his camp on the western side, separated by the river Orontes. Unbeknown to him, his opponent, the Hittite monarch Muwatallis, had already reached Kadesh. When the first Egyptian division was settling down, the Hittite king sent his fast-moving chariots across the river westwards and sliced through the marching second division of Pre. The enemy troops swung quickly to the north and attacked the Egyptian bivouac. Thus commenced a major battle for the control of the region of Amurru in southern Syria.

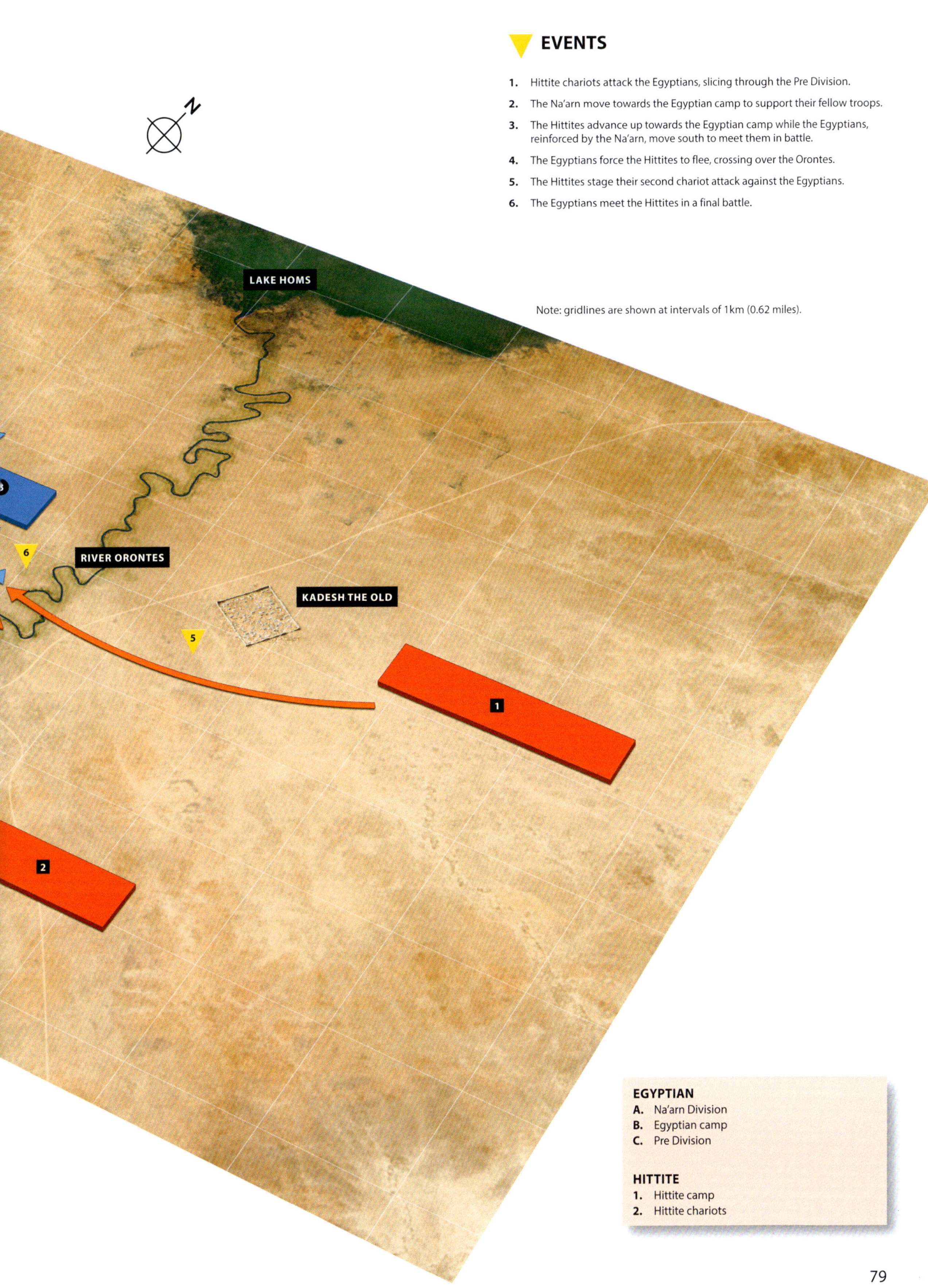

EVENTS

1. Hittite chariots attack the Egyptians, slicing through the Pre Division.
2. The Na'arn move towards the Egyptian camp to support their fellow troops.
3. The Hittites advance up towards the Egyptian camp while the Egyptians, reinforced by the Na'arn, move south to meet them in battle.
4. The Egyptians force the Hittites to flee, crossing over the Orontes.
5. The Hittites stage their second chariot attack against the Egyptians.
6. The Egyptians meet the Hittites in a final battle.

Note: gridlines are shown at intervals of 1km (0.62 miles).

EGYPTIAN

A. Na'arn Division
B. Egyptian camp
C. Pre Division

HITTITE

1. Hittite camp
2. Hittite chariots

combat and just before the written account of the Poem. It is thus the coda to the entire conflict. At Karnak, K2 does the same. Hence, the last rites of battle visually end all association with Kadesh. The events suit a time after the conclusion of hostilities and the cleaning of the field.

CONCLUSION: DAY ONE

The Poem alone provides us with useful facts relating to the day's end, but it still does not mention the whereabouts of the divisions of Ptah and Seth. How significant was the second wave of chariots is equally a puzzle. To himself, Ramesses was the victor and nothing more mattered; a great victory occurred when he drove the enemy chariots into the Orontes. No specifics are given for the second phase of chariot fighting, and one can ask whether Muwatallis' forces were that large after all.

Near sunset, Ramesses' army came to praise him. This section offers the exclamations or ovations of the soldiers to the pharaoh when they reached the camp (P 224–234). If the soldiers belonged to the third and fourth divisions, this would imply a rapid victory of Ramesses over the Hittites in phase two of the fighting. Just before this, there is a notation of the field covered with dead men with a reference to the high officials and chariotry praising their lord. Only later in P 251 and following does a fuller mention appear of the contingents on the Egyptian side. At that juncture, Ramesses addresses his infantry, high officials and chariotry. The Egyptian king is given a further occasion to berate his troops, a very unfair vituperation. It is worthwhile to mention that when Ramesses praises the few who proved loyal, no high official is indicated.

In this spiteful denunciation of cowardice, Ramesses now refers to the present danger which he and his troops had experienced. This time he turns to the actual experiences in battle, as the aim is to chastise his troops in regard to what will occur in the future. Then he mentions the only three groups who had supported him: the horses, the butlers and Menna. These are the only ones who were 'at my side', as the Poem indicates. Hence, Ramesses continues to stress his isolation from the main body of soldiers up to the end.

THE SECOND DAY

The composition then turns to the opening actions of the second day, when the land 'turned bright' and Ramesses marshalled his troops. The narrative implies that combat was expected to take place as soon as it was possible. We cannot but assume that he and Muwatallis had agreed in some way upon fighting. Otherwise, the reconstruction of events would have to assume that the enemy found it easy to cross over the Orontes and engage their opponent in the field without any immediate opposition.

The evidence concerning the follow-up clash on the second day has frequently been glossed over or misunderstood. Ramesses would have had enough troops to withstand any Hittite charge westwards unless the military interplay of both war leaders was that there would be an agreement upon encounter. How else could Muwatallis have forced Ramesses to additional fighting? His first two attacks had failed and he lost many of his men as well as war vehicles in both clashes. In addition, he would easily have been hindered if he chose to cross the Orontes yet again, as Ramesses' troops were well prepared for combat at dawn. I earlier concluded that some type of a 'show of force' encounter occurred on day two, one that was predetermined by both war leaders to take place in the open field. Otherwise, how can we understand that third clash?

The account of the Poem is as epically rhetorical as could be and provides nothing to grasp. The fighting concluded with a message being sent from the east to the west in which Muwatallis urged Ramesses to opt for peace. Granted the orientation of the Poem, once more the Hittite king appears to have avoided fighting personally. But there is nothing essential in the narrative of the Poem for the second day. The sequence is uncomplicated:

a. The sun began to rise. It was a clear day for fighting. Ramesses is not described as entering the enemy host 'at a gallop', as he did more than once on the previous day, because he was no longer surprised, trapped or in danger.
b. Ramesses then marshalled his troops.
c. He then fought.
d. Clearly, a Hittite force was opposite him. No information is presented as to where the place of combat was. How the enemy got across the Orontes, for this must be assumed, is not explained.
e. Ramesses defeated his opponents.
f. The Hittites stood away from the melee and attempted to surrender. P 290–293 is somewhat ambiguous:

> Then they [the enemy troops] began to take their stand,
> afar off, kissing the earth with their hands in front of me.
> Then my majesty prevailed over them, I killing them.
> I did not relax, they being prostrate in front of my
> horses.

This is definitely the final combat that the Egyptian king engaged in, and it is very peculiar. It would appear that enemy soldiers saw themselves defeated, or at least stymied, and started to implore for peace, only to endure a bit further the combative nature of Ramesses.

Mutawallis then dispatched his envoy to Ramesses asking for peace. There were actually two separate contacts. The first occasion took place when Muwatallis must have known that his army had failed on the second day: 'Then the vile, fallen chief of Hatti sent paying honor' (P 295–296). An oral statement would have sufficed for this preliminary act of the enemy leader, but an official note would fit the scenario, especially as Muwatallis was still positioned on the east of the Orontes. Subsequently, Muwatallis 'had his messenger come carrying a document' (P 300). This is the official written agreement of the end of combat. The letter would have included precise stipulations to arrange the agreement.

This resulted in the end of fighting. Ramesses then called together his highest officers and the leaders of the chariotry and infantry. A formal setting is presumed in which the words of the opponent were read out and the result was agreed upon. The army then prepared for departure. There was an official ceremony of triumph in the field, the counting of the dead and so forth. Unfortunately, this remains somewhat unclear as to timing, but it probably occurred on day two after all combat had ceased. The conclusion to the first day's fighting was close enough to the onset of evening twilight to prevent such a major celebratory event. Did Ramesses then leave, or perhaps stay there overnight? Unfortunately, any precise chronological dating is speculative.

The second day's confrontation parallels the expected battlefield topos that the Egyptian encounters followed when their large armies advanced upon various metropolises in Asia. The scenario on day two belongs to the 'accepted' standard of New Kingdom war narratives: pharaoh advances upon a city, a battle then ensues – normally within one day after arrival – and the enemy capitulates. The expectation was that combat had to occur on an open field or plain, located outside of the citadel. The metropolis opposed the Egyptians but could not expect to win. Some show of force was necessary. The ensuing fight was ludic, fought to demonstrate honourable resistance.

This situation of 'a flourish for the sake of bravado' fits well with the 'pharaoh ludens' remarks of Erik Hornung. Such fighting was somewhat ritualized. This must have been the situation on day two at Kadesh. Otherwise, how can we explain that rather odd, yet hyperbolic, narrative in the Poem as well as the background of the clash in the early morning. Both sides needed to arrange their troops.

Some type of permission to cross over was offered by Ramesses, or else he was too weak to prevent a third advance. We can assume that the Hittites were once more mainly, if not totally, chariot based. Additional time must then be allowed for Muwatallis to send his footsoldiers south, bypassing Kadesh and then advancing to the ford. Or one might want to reconstruct the Hittite advance moving westwards directly from Kadesh the Old to the base camp of the Egyptians.

So long as Muwatallis remained in control of the west, a clash was still inevitable unless one side was too weak to proceed. One cannot but conclude that the confrontation was not as ferocious, long lasting or severe as seen on the previous day. Thus a *homo ludens* military encounter, arranged and represented by both monarchs, took place. Ramesses, in fact, no longer had the military wherewithal to conduct a siege, much less to charge over to the Hittite zone and attack his enemy.

The official letter, written on a clay tablet in Akkadian or orally declared, was the overture from the Hittites for the cessation of active combat. It must have included the obvious condition that Ramesses could do what he wished in departing from the arena of conflict. Muwatallis had failed to annihilate Ramesses in the first wave and subsequently was unable to dislodge him from possession of the field, but the Hittites still retained control over Kadesh. Neither side felt that it possessed the strength to defeat the other, but the strategic victory was Muwatallis'. Ramesses left the area, but when remains unclear. It may have been on the next day, although this remains speculative.

The battle of Kadesh severely limited Ramesses' ability to retake the southern region of Syria. He never did. But departing from the field did not mean that the active hostilities between Hatti and Egypt had ceased. The Egyptians still possessed enough military strength to extend the conflict for years thereafter until a peace treaty was finally concluded in the 21st regnal year of Ramesses.

ANALYSIS

The military parameters of this battle can now be summarized and more deeply explicated. First and foremost, the encounter was unexpected. Neither opponent had prepared for this clash even though both assumed that any major combat would have to involve both kings and many troops. Ramesses knew that Mutawallis was already prepared for bloodshed and had assembled a very large army with reinforcements sent from the north-west. Both Ramesses and Muwatallis were limited by the logistic nature of Syria: they had to advance with their soldiers along the well-traversed age-old highways. As a result, the two opponents needed above all to know exactly where their foe was.

The main force, led by Ramesses, was to come up through the central valley system of Palestine and then proceed in a slightly north-east direction west of the citadel of Kadesh. His route was well known to his foe, and that is why the supposition that Hittite observers were scouring the area around Kadesh makes excellent sense. Muwatallis, who had arrived at the city earlier, had already dispatched his 'foot intelligence agency' to find out where Ramesses was. We do not know when the Hittite ruler arrived at Kadesh. Had some additional time passed between setting up his camp and Ramesses' arrival? I believe that since Muwatallis had effectively positioned his troops, assuredly sent others in hiding to the ford and stayed ensconced yet protected behind Kadesh the Old, he was extremely well prepared. In addition, he appears to have been situated roughly on the same level as Ramesses' bivouac and thus could have received news of the first military clash relatively quickly.

Muwatallis had effectively determined when to hit the second division of Pre, just as he had earlier avoided attacking Ramesses' number one division. Would it not have been easier to cut the head off the body as soon as possible? I suspect that he was careful not to be hit by the next large Egyptian cohort marching not far away from the first. By allowing his opponent to begin to settle down in camp (see R 11), Muwatallis expertly propelled his chariots across the ford to intersect the second hostile force when it was exposed in marching. Thus it is probable that the Hittite king knew what to do owing to a well-organized spy service.

But Ramesses was not bereft of military intelligence. His move to Kadesh was not accomplished in a daze, lacking calculation and planning. The Na'arn, separate from the rest, was to cut across the southern zone of Syria from the coast and then meet up with the king. It is clear that the encampment was to be to the west of the Orontes and that none of the Egyptian troops would cross over it when arriving. But it seems reasonable that Ramesses first expected to engage in a battle outside of Kadesh and then, at the worst, to effect a siege, but not against the Hittites.

The attack of Muwatallis totally changed the fighting. A combined infantry–chariotry force coupled with archer components never came into serious play by either side. Muwatallis initially relied on speed and thus was committed to a full chariot attack. Ramesses, caught in his camp, was rescued by the Na'arn, who gave him enough time to re-form his troops for combat. The Egyptians ended up possessing both infantry and chariotry in their initial repulse of the enemy. During the initial stages of fighting, the momentum – and thus greater fighting power – was in the hands of the Hittite chariot warriors. But by the time that the united division of Na'arn entered the fray, Ramesses had a distinct advantage. The enemy chariots were still spread out around the field and camp, whereas the Na'arn were not.

Since the core of the first phase involved chariots on one side and at the beginning somewhat of a mixture on the other, one can argue that the lack of reinforcements doomed the Hittites to failure. They were effective at first, startling and decisive in eliminating the Egyptian second division. In camp, Ramesses' life was at stake. He was isolated, even though troops were always there to support him. Observe that he had enough time to discover what happened in the south; i.e., the immobilization and dispersal of the division of Pre. Ramesses was already deeply in discussion with his officers when the enemy chariots moved across the river.

How could Muwatallis have expected to annihilate Ramesses? The first time would have been when he left the pharaoh isolated. But previously, Muwatallis had the opportunity to capture Ramesses on the march north. He did not do this owing to the proximity of the second Egyptian division. That body of troops, however, had then to be removed from the chess board, and this was done with surgical precision. It may be supposed that Muwatallis was unaware of the fifth division advancing eastwards, although this speculation remains unsure. I feel that he knew that time was of the essence. The Hittite chariots had to reach Ramesses and dispatch all in the bivouac as quickly as possible. If not, then the Egyptians could form a coherent, sizeable host able to defend themselves from any threat.

The resistance of the Egyptians proved to be effective owing to the Na'arn. Ramesses managed to regroup his entrapped troops because the enemy chariots had yet to arrive en masse and in large numbers. Ramesses had enough time to save himself and begin to prepare for battle. The Na'arn gave him the breathing space to reassemble. Muwatallis eventually saw (or heard of) the adverse pressure on his own forces and so sent, again without opposition, additional chariots. The arrival of the Na'arn had neutralized the initial Hittite threat, and with the reestablishment of military order, cohesion and leadership returned rather fast. These fresh soldiers added the necessary support to what was left of the first division and so enabled Ramesses to effect a counter-offensive. The enemy chariots thus found themselves in a quandary. In the end, they needed infantry support, and this is what Muwatallis must have realized but could not supply owing to time constraints. Therefore, the Hittite ruler had need of another fast counterblow; and with his own forces of phase one now on the defensive, he acted.

Throughout the extensive battle we can ascertain the relatively short amount of time for each decisive act on the part of the two antagonists. Muwatallis relied heavily on the velocity of his chariots from the very beginning. In reaction, his Egyptian opponent had little time to defend himself at his camp and needed breathing space. The latter was supplied by the Na'arn who, at least to scholars, appeared on the horizon in the right place and at the right time. The clash that immediately ensued still required the pharaoh's personal leadership as well as some regrouping of his prime division.

This too had to occur quickly. Subsequently, Muwatallis, 'looking at the fighting of his majesty' (P 144), again had to dispatch another group of chariots as soon as possible. A serious criticism of historical reconstruction dealing with the latter phase of fighting centres upon the timing of this decision. We do not know when the Hittite king would have decided that reinforcements had to be sent in order to stop the Egyptian counter-attack. Whether this was caused by his knowledge that Ramesses' push back was highly successful, and that the elite chariot troops were being relentlessly shoved into the Orontes, is part speculation, part common sense. Muwatallis may have decided that his chariots needed more support irrespective of how the first wave's host was doing.

Ramesses, on the other hand, extricated himself from the enemy penetration of his camp. This indicates that the Na'arn division was ready at hand, not at all settling down for rest, and was able to launch its own chariot counter-attack. Furthermore, only the very close Hittite war vehicles appear to have reached the Egyptians, even though we can see, following the pictorial sources of the first episode, that some were within the camp. To repeat, it would appear that the king quickly prepared to fight and then sent his chariots speedily forward into the melee. He still had enough breathing space. The second phase ended when the enemy had ceased to fight, but whether the remaining Hittites and their allies asked for peace is another matter. Actually, only their monarch could do so; and by the end of day, he was not yet willing to cease hostilities.

Muwatallis was prepared for a resumption of combat, and the events on the following day, ludic though they appear to modern-day readers, bear witness to his determination to continue the contest. Ramesses, who in the final analysis held the field, felt the same way. In his case, however, although he held full control of the field west of the river, he could not dislodge the Hittites from their side. He had additional reinforcements in the third and fourth divisions, and this no doubt encouraged him to pursue the conflict. But his as well as Muwatallis' point of view on the second day essentially were based on a ludic concept of a military contest. Yet we can grant to Ramesses the expectation that, with two intact southerly divisions, he might, after all, be able to win, possibly on the morrow. Yet Muwatallis knew otherwise, and he never crossed the river to the west. Evidently, the Hittite king was content to remain on the eastern bank. One suspects that he knew that he was in a better situation than Ramesses, despite his losses on day one.

The Hittite ruler wisely kept many of his soldiers near him – the teher are the most famous – and purposely set himself up at Kadesh the Old more to the east rather than at the city of Kadesh. In fact, by using the ford to the south of both cities, Muwatallis was even farther away and thus better positioned to form some type of retreat or set up a strongly defended redoubt in case of a successful monumental Egyptian attack. But Ramesses never crossed that river eastwards, proof that, unambiguously, he had not the strength to do so.

AFTERMATH

There still are questions affecting the immediate and the long-range effects that Ramesses' withdrawal had on the relations between both superpowers. The first is regarding the evacuation from the field and the pharaoh's return to Egypt. However ebullient and splendid the official written account of the Poem may be, there is no gainsaying that he lost the battle. Many evaluations temper that sharp conclusion by stating that Ramesses won the battle but lost the field. Actually, this evaluation is incorrect. It is further assumed that Hittite forces chased Egyptians out of the land of Aba (around Damascus, south of Kadesh) and then Muwatallis appointed a certain Hattusilis (III) – son of Mursilis II, the elder brother of Muwatallis and the future king – as plenipotentiary over that city. But the coincidence of the two events – the battle of Kadesh, the takeover of Aba – are not conclusively linked and the chronology is unclear on this matter. Yet there is little doubt that Aba remained firmly under Hittite control with Hattusilis III in charge. As an aside, he saw action at Kadesh. It is only from Hittite sources that we learn of this. (He was commander of the infantry and chariotry.)

We must consider exactly what success and failure in war mean, both to an individual and to the collective. Ramesses' goal was to re-secure Kadesh for himself, to place it under Egyptian control after many years. As always, it was the key to southern Syria as well as to the routes leading both north and east. This was not obtained. Hence, Ramesses lost. It is true that the two chariot attacks of the Hittites did not succeed in defeating him or even dislodging the Egyptian army from the area. Ramesses still remained on the west side of the Orontes at the time of sunset on the first day. Even if the evidence as to the ramifications of the clash is murky, it is fair to conclude that Muwatallis was unable to weaken his foe sufficiently to force the Egyptian king to surrender.

But the same may be said for the other side. Ramesses could not cross over the river to the east – the arrival of the third and fourth divisions notwithstanding – and even if the fighting on the second day was inconclusive – either undertaken as a ludic performance or as a distinct and honourable 'show of force' – it nevertheless provided nothing positive for the pharaoh. Hence, when all is said and done, Ramesses lost. He retreated, having obtained nothing. On the other side, I suspect that the Hittite king was too weakened after the first day to attempt a definitive combat success, or any type of convincing victory, on the following morning. Thus it is highly probable that a *modus vivendi* was achieved and the Egyptians departed.

In the next few years, the pharaoh returned to this area but Ramesses never approached Kadesh. He stuck to the southern zone of Hittite domination and inland rather than the coast. (For example, the Egyptians never reached as far north as Ugarit.) The war records are pictorial and hence have to be viewed from a vantage point quite different from that of written accounts, especially as the scenes are of a common military nature, attacking cities on tells (mounds). There are no snapshots of victory which indicate that Ramesses ever again fought against an army that was personally directed by the ruling monarch of Hatti. None of the pictorial representations indicate a coalition of lands opposing the Egyptians. Rather, they reveal a persistent attempt of Ramesses to gain small pieces of land on the borders of territory aligned to the Hittites but not directly ruled by Muwatallis. But on the other side, the Hittite monarch replaced the prince of Amurru, Benteshina, and deported him to Hatti. That country was now permanently pro-Hittite. The key strategic port of Tell Kazel, Sumur, was forever blocked against Egyptian control.

There is an additional useful point to state. Ramesses originally had an ally in Benteshina. To be sure, while that man was later dethroned by Muwatallis, he was kept alive. In the meantime, the Kadesh texts specifically use the term 'Land of Amurru' twice (P 63 and R 19). It was there that Ramesses had stationed his fifth division, the Na'arn, right 'on the shore of the land of Amurru'. By doing so, the texts refer to the country of Amurru and not to the geographical zone. (In cuneiform, the two are differentiated by the terms 'Land of Amurru' = country and 'Lands of Amurru' = region/zone.) This contrast appears to be reflected here. Then too, Amurru, being on the side of Ramesses, is not listed at all within the Hittite confederacy.

The final stages of conflict saw a winding down of both direct and indirect confrontation. Internal difficulties in the lands of the Hittites were connected to royal succession. A long-range process of stability between the two powers culminated in a peace treaty that was finally approved in Ramesses' 21st regnal year. By that time, all attempts by Ramesses to influence Hatti came to naught, even if he had, purely by chance, supported Urkhi-Teshub, the son and successor of Muwatallis, when Hattusilis III, his uncle, seized power in Anatolia. Hattusilis III had no intention of expanding southwards and originally was content to keep Urkhi-Teshub in Syria. He was then sent to Amurru for conspiring with Babylon. Benteshina was king of Amurru once more. It is highly probable that Urkhi-Teshub remained for a while 'along the seashore', to quote a cuneiform document which uses a geographic passage that remarkably echoes two earlier Egyptian Kadesh reports that place the Na'arn in Amurru, with one specifically adding 'upon the shore', thereby perhaps indicating the key port of Sumur, Tell Kazel (P 63 and R 19). Urkhi-Teshub finally fled to Egypt. But all of that was after the peace treaty between Ramesses and the Hittite king Hattusilis III. Insofar as neither monarch wished to engage in outright war in Syria continually, the two rulers made peace. One can also argue that the Egyptians had become more cognizant of a military threat from the west, from the Libyans, and so preferred to maintain their control over Palestine and a few outlying regions in Syria rather than to spend time and effort in campaigning so far in the north, where their success would be always moot, to say the least.

The battle of Kadesh had not, however, ended Hittite–Egyptian hostilities. It took at least seven or so years for the Egyptians to realize their impotence in the area of the province state of Amurru and to understand that the best policy was that of a cold war. But the results of the battle were obvious. Ramesses could not claim any more newly won or retaken territory north of his Palestinian client states. On the other hand, the armed engagement resolved matters that neither opponent would, or indeed could, realize. First, it did decide, and on the spot, that Egypt would never conquer Amurru. Neither foe knew this, even after Ramesses departed from the city. Second, it effectively left the Hittites in control of Syria, with the challenge of the growing power of Assyria. It did not end their jockeying for power in the region, although the failure of Ramesses effectively removed one of the contenders in the Great Game of Syria. Henceforth, only Hatti and Assyria held the cards.

The ultimate result of this famous military contest in regnal year five of Ramesses II was to prevent him, and thus the strength of Egypt, from ever crossing over into the Syrian lands abutting the northern zone of Palestine. It meant that Egypt could no longer even advance to the Euphrates, as it had been done under Thutmose III. Perhaps more significantly, it finally defined the northern limit of Egyptian domination. In essence, the lines of political control had become rigid.

One final evaluation is necessary at the end of this discussion: it is necessary to have an expert and up-to-date intelligence service at your fingertips. All commanders need information, and even from the biased accounts of the Egyptian side, it is strikingly evident that Ramesses was not well served in this sphere. His wish for posterity to believe that it was others who were to blame – administrators and the like – does not ring true, even if the underlying causes for this major failure on his part cannot be fathomed too deeply because we are not given any data concerning those foreign officials and the allied locals who could – and should – have known better. In similar fashion, to blame your troops for cowardice appears, even so far removed in time from the battle, to be stretching the historical events too much. The first division was caught unawares, and that cannot be ignored. The charioteers in the bivouac could not, for the most part, have been able to reach their vehicles rapidly owing to the sudden arrival and attack of their enemies. Therefore, it is to be expected that they could do little except flee. Ramesses' local infantry, as I have pointed out, were in a better shape to effect resistance to Muwatallis' chariot charge. After all, they just needed to take their weapons and form themselves into small bands, refusing either to flee or to surrender. But I do feel that Ramesses was inherently correct in viewing his troops of the A-plus division which he personally led, that of Amun, as having failed to support him when the crisis came.

His remarks concerning the lack of backing from (shall we say) almost anyone that permeate the compositions written as a personal report on his 'victory' are more understandable when it is realized that this theme of betrayal is connected to the parallel one of loyalty. That is why I consider the plea to Amun by the solitary Ramesses to be less religiously oriented and less pietistic than argued by Assmann. I feel that the sense of loyalty permeates the entire composition of the Poem and is what one would expect from any military-oriented report on a battle. All soldiers, armed cohorts of men, expect full and unquestionable support from their comrades, be they generals or grunts. Armies do not merely survive, but frequently win through the morale of their troops. Generalship, indeed leadership, depends upon faithfulness, fealty and fidelity. Ramesses points out that he has shown these traits unfailingly and unflinchingly to Amun, but his troops have not done the same to him. Thus at the very end, Ramesses still berates his soldiers when 'they' – of course, not everyone – come back to his encampment at dusk. That is why he purposely ignores them when he praises his butlers – whom we never read as engaging in battle – chariot horses and Menna.

Yet it is somewhat conspicuous that Ramesses, in the Poem as well as in the Bulletin, never praises the Na'arn. This absence is particularly notable at the end of the first day's account when they are not included in the list of supporters. I can give no reason for this but remark, as many do, that the Na'arn appear on the horizon in the moderately lengthy caption of R 11. Yet that mention remains a solitary one, save a brief remark in the Poem (P 63–64), and even there the designation 'Na'arn' is lacking. It does appear that Ramesses is just too egotistical, too distraught with his army and lacking in balance to have a fairer account written. On the other hand, such was not the purpose of the Poem.

Muwatallis, in contrast, appears to have been blessed with luck. But that simple explanation disregards his careful planning and, earlier, his use of spies and scouts. He most definitely had been at Kadesh for more than one day preceding Ramesses' arrival. How much he knew of his opponent's structure of forces – the layout of the four divisions – is anyone's guess. I do not believe that he was aware of the proximity of the Na'arn, because if so, his chariot attack at the Egyptian camp would be a very precarious venture. On the other hand, he certainly knew when to isolate the first division by incapacitating the army of Pre by using the ford across the Orontes. The Hittite monarch must have had his own spies circulating on the east and west sides of the Orontes, to the north and south, in order to ferret out the enemy's positions. I strongly believe that he kept his 'eye' – that is, his agents did – upon the advance of the Egyptian troops as they moved northwards from a little south of Shabtuna. Muwatallis did, after all, send his chariots westwards at a very opportune time, when the third and fourth divisions were not in the vicinity and the first was settling down.

The Hittite king further showed his tactical strategic intelligence by using the fast-moving vehicles to incapacitate the division of Pre. He purposely avoided sending any infantry onto the field, and this policy worked perfectly. It almost annihilated Ramesses and most certainly put out of commission his second division. Moreover, he had possession of the field, as is seen perfectly when he dispatched the second wave of chariots. They met with no opposition until they encountered the Egyptians in the north. When he was frustrated, Muwatallis did not lose heart. Even after the second half of the day's battle came to a close, he remained secure in his well-planned bivouac at Kadesh the Old.

Muwatallis' strategic sense was as keen as his tactical awareness. He deliberately placed himself at quite a distance from the ford of the Orontes. In addition, his encampment was situated a bit farther to the east, meaning it would be very difficult for an outsider to perceive his location. The chariots had been moved south to Kadesh. Whether this was done at the start – i.e., when Ramesses' first division was in sight or earlier – remains moot. P 70–71 of the Poem nonetheless indicate that Muwatallis had already stationed his chariots – just them – behind Kadesh itself. Hence, I believe that this was done soon before the division of Amun was in sight of the Hittite scouts. Muwatallis was biding his time, waiting for a feeling that all was perfect to attack. He depended upon his perception of the main Egyptian army of four divisions, and even if he was unaware of the last one, that of Seth, I suspect that he was fully cognizant of the division of Ptah, so far strung out in the south. His surprise charge across the Orontes appears to have relied on that intelligence-gathering service which he had already placed in the field. By doing so, he could receive desired news about his foe as quickly as was possible at that time. Both the first and second chariot charges indicate well-planned yet fast decision making.

In contrast to the Hittite ruler, Ramesses personally engaged in this military struggle. Whereas Muwatallis remained to the east, from the start the pharaoh took up arms, first to protect himself and his troops and then to carry the combat into the heart of the chariot thrust. We cannot but give total credit to him for showing complete determination and strength when it at first appeared that his camp would be completely destroyed. With the support of his army, of course, Ramesses stood – and still does stand – as a heroic figure in combat. He managed to turn an extremely dangerous threat into a success in the field. How much of his eventual battlefield victory on the first day was due to the limited resources of his Hittite opponent cannot be ascertained to any strict degree. To take a case in point: how many effective enemy chariots did Muwatallis send across the Orontes on the two separate occasions? Was the location of the fighting north of the ford somewhat too far removed, thereby allowing the Egyptians to prepare a better defence at first and a victory on the second day? After all, the first chariot onslaught upon Ramesses was not organized well enough to achieve his annihilation. That is to say, were the Hittite chariots, attacking by themselves, pushing ahead without any tightly knit coordination? If so, a concerted defence at the camp could effectively resist the pressure for enough time to allow the Na'arn their own charge. It can be claimed that this fifth division was well coordinated to attack, whereas the Hittite chariot thrust was dependent upon a quick immobilization of their opponents – if that were not possible, then the conflict would become a melee of fast-moving forces versus a well-organized cohort of infantry and chariotry.

However one reinterprets the phases of the battle of Kadesh, and argues over and over concerning the possible outcomes that might have taken place, this two-day conflict was momentous and decisive. It did not end the warfare between Hatti and Egypt, but it effectively put an end to Ramesses' wish to secure some control over the southernmost zone of Syria, including the coast, and especially the city of Kadesh. It was, indeed, the decisive battle in the New Kingdom because it put an end to further northern Egyptian imperialism.

BIBLIOGRAPHY

Abbas, M., 'The Bodyguard of Ramesses II and the Battle of Kadesh' in *Égypte Nilotique et Méditerranéenne* 9, Université Paul-Valéry, Montpellier, pp.113–23 (2016)

Assmann, J., 'Krieg und Frieden im alten Ägypten. Ramses II. und die Schlacht bei Kadesch' in *Mannheimer Forum*, Vol. 83/84, Universität Mannheim, Mannheim, pp.174–231 (1984)

Beal, R., 'Hittite Military Organization' in J. Sasson (ed.), *Civilizations of the Ancient Near East* I, Scribner, New York, pp.545–54 (1995)

Beal, R., *The Organization of the Hittite Military*, C. Winter, Heidelberg (1992)

Brand, P., *Ramesses II: Egypt's Ultimate Pharaoh*, Lockwood Press, Columbus, GA (2024)

Brand P., *The Monuments of Seti I. Epigraphic, Historical & Art Historical Analysis*, Brill, Leiden (2000)

Brownrigg, G., 'Harnessing the Chariot Horse' in P. Raulwing, K. M. Linduff & J. H. Crouwel (eds), *Equids and Wheeled Vehicles in the Ancient World: Essays in Memory of Mary A. Littauer*, BAR Publishing, Oxford, pp.85–96 (2019)

Bryce, T., *Hittite Warrior*, Osprey, Oxford (2007)

Bryce, T., *The Kingdom of the Hittites* (new edition), Clarendon Press, Oxford (2005)

Carter, H. & Newberry, P. E., *The Tomb of Thoutmôsis IV*, Archibald Constable and Co., Westminster (1904)

Cavillier, G., *La battaglia di Qadesh: Ramesse II alla conquista dell'Asia, fra Mito, storia e strategi*, Tirrenia Stampatori, Turin (2006)

Champollion, J.-F., *Monuments de l'Égypte et de la Nubia* I, Didot, Paris (1844)

Crouwel, J. H., 'Studying the Six Chariots from the tomb of Tutankhamun' in A. J. Veldmeijer & S. Ikram (eds), *Chasing Chariots: Proceedings of the First International Chariot Conference (Cairo 2012)*, Sidestone Press, Leiden, pp.73–93 (2013)

Darnell, J., 'Kadesh' in J. Powell (ed.), *Magill's Guide to Military History*, Salem Press, Pasedena, CA, p.814 (2001)

Darnell, J. & Manassa, C., *Tutankhamun's Armies: Battle and Conquest during Ancient Egypt's Late 18th Dynasty*, John Wiley & Sons, Hoboken, NJ (2007)

Degrève, A., 'La campagne asiatique de l'an 1 de Séthy Ier représentée sur le mur extérieur nord de la salle hypostyle du temple d'Amon à Karnak' in *Revue d'Égyptologie*, Vol. 57, Société française d'égyptologie, Paris, pp.47–76 (2006)

Delbrück, H., *Numbers in History*, University of London Press, London (1913)

Epigraphic Survey, *Reliefs and Inscriptions at Karnak* IV, University of Chicago Press, Chicago, IL (1979)

Gaballa, G. A., *Narrative in Egyptian Art*, von Zabern, Mainz am Rhein (1976)

Gardiner, A., *The Kadesh Inscriptions of Ramesses II*, Griffith Institute, Oxford (1960)

Gerván, H., 'La representación de Ramsés II en escenas del corpus iconográfico de la batalla de Kadesh: argumentos semióticos para una "continuidad intersticial" en el plano onto-semántico' in *Boletín de la Asociación Española de Egiptología*, Vol. 29, Asociación Española de Egiptología, Madrid, pp.77–118 (2020)

Goedicke, H. (ed.), *Perspectives on the Battle of Kadesh*, Halgo, Baltimore, MD (1985)

Goelet, O. & Iskander, S., *Temple of Ramesses II in Abydos. Volume 1: Wall Scenes – Part I: Exterior Walls and Courts*, Lockwood Press, Atlanta, GA (2015)

Gnirs, A., *Militär und Gesellschaft: ein Beitrag zur Sozialgeschichte des Neuen Reiches*, Heidelberger Orientverlag, Heidelberg (1996)

Haider, P. W., 'Troia zwischen Hethitern, Mykenern, und Mysern. Besitzt der Troianische Krieg einen historischen Hintergrund?' in H. D. Galter (ed.), *Troia, Mythen und Archäologie*, Grazer Morgenländische Studien, Graz, pp.97–140 (1997)

Hansen, K., 'Collection in Ancient Egyptian Chariot Horses' in *Journal of the American Research Center in Egypt*, Vol. 29, Lockwood Press, Columbus, GA, pp.173–79 (1992)

Hartman, T. C., *The Kadesh Inscriptions of Rameses II: An Analysis of the Verbal Patterns of a Ramesside Royal Inscription*, Brandeis University PhD Thesis, Waltham, MA (1967)

Hawkins, J. D., 'The Political Geography of Arzawa (Western Anatolia)' in N. C. Stampolidis, C. Maner & K. Kopanias (eds), *Nostoi. Indigenous Culture, Migration and Integration in the Aegean Islands and Western Anatolia during the Late Bronze and Early Iron Age*, Koç University Press, Istanbul, pp.15–35 (2015)

Heagren, B., *The Art of War in Pharaonic Egypt: An Analysis of the Tactical, Logistic, and Operational Capabilities of the Egyptian Army, Dynasties XVII–XX*, Auckland University PhD Thesis, Auckland (2010)

Heinz, S., *Die Feldzugdarstellungen des Neuen Reiches: Eine Bildanalyse*, Akademie der Wissenschaften, Vienna (2001)

Hornung, E., 'Pharaoh Ludens' in *Eranos Jahrbuch*, Vol. 51, Eranos Foundation, Ascona, pp.479–516 (1982)

Kenning, J., *Der Feldzug nach Kadesch: Das Ägypten des Neuen Reiches auf der Suche nach seiner Strategie*, Olms, Hildesheim, Zurich and New York (2014)

Kitchen, K. A., *Pharaoh Triumphant: The Life and Times of Ramesses II, King of Egypt*, Aris and Phillips, Warminster (1982)

Kitchen, K. A., *Ramesside Inscriptions: Historical and Biographical. Translations* II, Blackwell, Oxford and Cambridge, MA (1996)

Kitchen, K.A., *Ramesside Inscriptions: Translated and Annotated. Notes and Comments* II, Blackwell, Oxford and Malden, MA (1999)

Krauss, R., 'Über die L-förmigen Schattenuhren und die Schlacht von Megiddo' in *Studien zur altägyptischen Kultur*, Vol. 47, Helmut Buske, Hamburg, pp.149–76 (2018)

Kuschke, A., 'Das Terrain bei Qadeš und die Anmarschwege Ramses' II. Summarium einer ebenso kritischen wie selbstkritischen Bestandsaufnahme, vorwiegend im Hinblick auf die geographischen Gegebenheiten' in *Zeitschrift des Deutschen Palästina Vereins*, Vol. 95, Harrassowitz, Wiesbaden, pp.7–35 (1979)

Littauer, M. A., 'A 19th and 20th Dynasty Heroic Motif' in P. Raulwing (ed.), *Selected Writings on Chariots, other Early Vehicles, Ridings and Harness*, Brill, Leiden, Boston, MA, and Cologne, pp.136–40 (2002)

Littauer, M. A., 'The Military Use of the Chariot in the Aegean in the Late Bronze Age' in P. Raulwing (ed.), *Selected Writings on Chariots, other Early Vehicles, Ridings and Harness*, Brill, Leiden, Boston, MA, and Cologne, pp.74–99 (2002)

Littauer. M. A. & Crouwel, J. H., *Chariots and Related Equipment from the Tomb of Tutankhamun*, Griffith Institute, Oxford (1985)

Littauer, M. A. & Crouwel, J. H., *Wheeled Vehicles and Ridden Animals in the Ancient Near East*, Brill, Leiden and Cologne (1979)

Lorenz, J. & Schrakamp, I., 'Hittite Military and Warfare' in H. Genz & D. P. Mielke (eds), *Insights into Hittite History and Archaeology*, Peeters, Leuven, Paris and Walpole, MA, pp.125–51 (2011)

Manassa, C., *Merneptah: Grand Strategy in the 13th Century* BC, Yale Egyptological Studies, New Haven, CT (2003)

Masters, K., *Pharaoh's Chariot Wheel in the 18th Dynasty: Its history, its mechanics, and its cultural relevance*, University of Manchester MA Thesis, Manchester (2022)

Morris, E., *Ancient Egyptian Imperialism*, Wiley-Blackwell, Hoboken, NJ (2018)

Nefedkin, A., 'On Typical Tactics of Oriental Chariot Battle' in *The Ancient History Bulletin*, Vol. 19.1–2, St Olaf College, Northfield, MN, pp.1–14 (2005)

Noblecourt, C. D., Donadoni, S. & Edel, E., *Grand temple d'Abou Simbel: La bataille de Qadech*, Centre de Documentation et d'études sur l'ancienne Égypt, Cairo (1971)

Obsomer, C., 'La bataille de Qadech de Ramsès II. Les n'arin, sekou tepy et questions d'itinéraires' in C. Karshausen & C. Obsomer (eds), *De la Nubie à Qadech/From Nubia to Kadesh: La guerre dans l'Égypte ancienne/War in Ancient Egypt*, Safran, Brussels, pp.81–170 (2016)

Obsomer, C., 'Ramsès face aux événements de Qadech. Pourquoi deux récits officiels différents?' in N. Grimal & M. Baud (eds), *Événement, récit, historie official: Actes du colloque du Collège de France 2002*, Cybèle, Paris, pp.87–95 (2003)

Obsomer, C., *Ramsès II*, Pygmalion, Paris (2012)

Obsomer, C., 'Récits et images de la bataille de Qadech. En quoi Ramsès II transforma-t-il la réalité' in L. van Ypersele (ed.), *Imaginaires de guerre: L'histoire entre mythe et réalité*, Academia Bryulant, Louvain-la-Neuve, pp.339–67 (2003)

Oreshko, R., 'Geography of the Western Fringes; Gar(a)giša/Gargiya and the Lands of the Late Bronze Age Caria' in O. Henry & K. Konuk (eds), *KARIA ARKHAIA. La Carie, des origines à la période pré-hékatomnide*, Ege Yayinlari, Istanbul, pp.139–89 (2019)

Parker, R. A., 'Some Reflections on the Lunar Dates of Thutmose III and Ramesses II' in W. K. Simpson & W. Davis (eds), *Studies in Ancient Egypt, the Aegean, and the Sudan: Essays in Honor of Dows Dunham on the Occasion of his 90th birthday, June 1, 1980*, Museum of Fine Arts, Boston, pp.146–47 (1981)

Parr, P. J. (ed.), *Excavations at Tell Neb I Mend, Syria. Volume I*, Oxbow, Oxford and Philadelphia (2015)

Prisse d'Avennes, A., *Histoire de l'art égyptien d'après les monuments* II, Arthus Bertrand, Paris (1878)

Rommelaere, C., *Les chevaux du Nouvel Empire égyptien: Origines, races, harnachement*, Connaissance de l'Égypte Ancienne, Paris (1991)

Rosellini, I., *Monumenti dell'Egitto e della Nubia, Monumenti storici* III, Niccolò Capura (1839)

Schulman, A., *Military Title, Rank, and Organization in the Egyptian New Kingdom*, Bruno Hessling, Berlin (1964)

Simon, Z., 'Against the Identification of Karkiša with Carians' in N. C. Stampolidis, C. Maner & K. Kopanias (eds), *Nostoi: Indigenous Culture, Migration and Integration in the Aegean Islands and Western Anatolia during the Late Bronze and Early Iron Age*, Koç University Press, Istanbul, pp.791–809 (2015)

Simon, Z., 'Die Lokalisierung von Karkiša' in S. Erkut & Ö. Gavaz (eds), *Studies in Honor of Ahmet Ünal Armagani*, Arkeoloji ve Sanat Yayinlar, Istanbul (2016), pp.255–68

Simon, Z., 'The Identification of Qode. Reconsidering the Evidence' in J. Mynářová (ed.), *Egypt and The Near East – The Crossroad*, Charles University in Prague, Czech Institute of Egyptology, Faculty of Arts, Prague, pp.249–69 (2011)

Singer, I., 'Syria after the Battle of Qadesh' in I. Singer, *The Calm before the Storm. Selected Writings of Itamar Singer on the Late Bronze Age in Anatolia and the Levant*, Society of Biblical Literature, Atlanta, GA, pp.3–17 (2011)

Singer, I., 'The "Land of Amurru" and the "Lands of Amurru" in the Šaušgamuwa Treaty' in *Iraq*, Vol. 53, British Institute for the Study of Iraq, London, pp.69–74 (1991)

Singer, I., 'The Urḫi-Teššub Affair in the Hittite-Egyptian Correspondence' in Th. van den Hout (ed.), *The Life and Times of Hattusili III and Tuthaliya IV*, Nederlands Instituut voor het Nabije Oosten, Leiden, pp.27–38 (2006)

Singer, I., 'Who were the Kaška?' in *Phasis. Greek and Roman Studies*, Vol. 10.1, Tbilisi State University, Tbilisi, pp.166–81 (2007)

Spalinger, A., 'Chariot Wheels' in *Studien zur altägyptischen Kultur*, Vol. 52, Helmut Buske, Hamburg, pp.241–53 (2023)

Spalinger, A., 'Divisions in Monumental Texts and their Images: The Issue of Kadesh and Megiddo' in M. Gruber et al. (eds), *All the Wisdom of the East. Studies in Honor of Eliezer D. Oren*, Academic Press and Vanderhoeck & Ruprecht, Fribourg and Göttingen, pp.373–93 (2012)

Spalinger, A., *Icons of Power: A Strategy of Reinterpretation*, Charles University of Prague, Faculty of Arts, Prague (2011)

Spalinger, A., *Leadership under Fire: The Pressures of Warfare in Ancient Egypt*, Soleb, Paris (2020)

Spalinger, A., 'Mathematical Factors of the Battle of Kadesh' in A. Spalinger, *Feasts and Fights. Essays on Time in Ancient Egypt*, Yale Egyptological Institute, New Haven, pp.89–107 (2018)

Spalinger, A., 'Notes on the Reliefs of the Battle of Kadesh' in H. Goedicke (ed.), *Perspectives on the Battle of Kadesh*, Halgo, Baltimore, MA, pp.1–42 (1985)

Spalinger, A., 'Points of View. Ramesses II and the Battle of Kadesh' in M. Abbas & F. Hoffmann (eds), *Perspectives on the Ramesside Military System. Proceedings of the International Conference Held at the Institute for Egyptology and Coptology of Ludwig-Maximilians-Universität, Munich, 10–11 December, 2021*, Zaphon, Münster, pp.157–85 (2023)

Spalinger, A., 'Ramesses Ludens et Alii' in K. Pangiotis (ed.), *Studies on the Ancient Egyptian Culture and Foreign Relations*, University of the Aegean, Rhodes, pp.71–86 (2007)

Spalinger, A., 'The Battle of Kadesh: The Chariot Frieze at Abydos' in *Ägypten und Levante* Vol. 13, Österreichische Akademie der Wissenschaften, Vienna, pp.163–99 (2001)

Spalinger, A., *The Books behind the Masks: Sources of Warfare Leadership in Ancient Egypt*, Brill, Leiden and Boston, MT (2021)

Spalinger, A., *The Transformation of an Ancient Egyptian Narrative: P. Sallier III and the Battle of Kadesh*, Harrassowitz, Wiesbaden (2002)

Spalinger, A., 'Trophies: Numbers and Locations', in preparation

Spalinger, A., *War in Ancient Egypt. The New Kingdom*, Blackwell, Oxford (2005)

Turner, S., *The Horse in New Kingdom Egypt: Its Introduction, Nature, Role and Impact*, Abercrombie Press, Wallasey (2023)

Veldmeijer, A. J. & Ikram, S. (eds), *Chariots in Ancient Egypt: The Tano Chariot, A Case Study*, Sidestone Press, Leiden (2018)

Veldmeijer, A. J. & Ikram, S. (eds), *Chasing Chariots: Proceedings of the First International Chariot Conference (Cairo 2012)*, Sidestone Press, Leiden (2013)

Von der Way, T., *Die Textüberlieferung Ramses' II: zur Qadeš-Schlacht*, Gerstenberger Verlag, Hildesheim (1984)

Weingartner, S., 'Some Observations on Chariotry and Chariot Warfare in the Near Eastern Late Bronze Age and the Battle of Kadesh' in P. Raulwing et al. (eds), *Chariots in Antiquity: Essays in Honour of Joost Crouwel*, BAR Publishing, Oxford, pp.273–312 (2023)

Wreszinski, Walter, *Atlas zur altägyptischen Kulturgeschichte* II, J. C. Hinrichs'schen Buchhandlung, Leipzig (1935)

INDEX

Figures in **bold** refer to illustrations.